The Successful Introvert

How to Enhance Your Job Search
and Advance Your Career

Wendy Gelberg

20660 Stevens Creek Blvd., Suite 210
Cupertino, CA 95014

Trademarks

Warning and Disclaimer

Endorsements

"My 'dirty little secret' is that I am an ultra-shy introvert (yes, I'm both; thank you Wendy Gelberg for explaining that they're not the same). Given that way of characterizing my personality, you can see that I've been socialized to believe shyness and introversion are bad. In reading just the first few passages in Wendy Gelberg's Introduction, I immediately saw myself, relaxed and felt better about my 'affliction,' and drank in her words: 'My goal in writing this book is to pick up where other job search and career transition books leave off and to honor people of all types.' She is so right — that no other career book is dedicated to people like us.

As a major proponent of using storytelling in the job search, I embraced Gelberg's strategy of changing/re-framing our shyness/introversion stories so they work in the job search. Wendy Gelberg GETS me, and she gets the multitudes of shy and/or introverted people like me, all of whom will benefit enormously from this unprecedented take on the job search. Wish I'd had this 30 years ago!"
Katharine Hansen, PhD, Associate Publisher and Creative Director, Quintessential Careers (http://quintcareers/com)

"What an immensely helpful book! Wendy has taken a fresh approach to a topic that is almost never mentioned in job search 'how-to' books. As an introvert myself, in my work as a career coach and résumé writer, I quickly recognize introversion in many of my clients and see first-hand how they struggle with many necessary job search tasks. Networking and interviewing can be painful for an introvert. But no more! I will recommend this book to every one of them. If you are an introvert, this book is a must read before beginning your next job search!"
**Michelle Dumas, Career Coach, Résumé Writer, and Personal Branding Strategist
Distinctive Career Services, LLC, http://distinctiveweb.com**

"Finally, a book targeted specifically to introverts and their unique challenges in today's job search market. Wendy offers sage advice, strategies, action plans and more to help you better manage your job search, interviews, negotiations and more. Follow her plan to career success!"
Wendy S. Enelow, CCM, MRW, JCTC, CPRW, Author & Executive Career Consultant

"If you're an introvert, you need this book! Because Gelberg truly understands the introverted personality, you will find great relief and sage advice for managing a job search in this seemingly extroverted world we live (and compete) in."
Susan Ireland (http://susanireland.com), Author, 'The Complete Idiot's Guide to the Perfect Resume'

"This book is very insightful and necessary in a world filled with personal interactions. Those who consider themselves introverts will be relieved that they share this same attribute as others, yet Wendy proves it's not exactly a bad thing. By reading this book, you will gain the self-awareness to make a difference in your life, secure the job of your dreams and become a better person."
Dan Schawbel, Publisher, Personal Branding Magazine

A Message from Happy About®

Thank you for your purchase of this Happy About book. It is available online at http://happyabout.info/thesuccessfulintrovert.php or at other online and physical bookstores.

- Please contact us for quantity discounts at sales@happyabout.info
- If you want to be informed by e-mail of upcoming Happy About® books, please e-mail bookupdate@happyabout.info

Happy About is interested in you if you are an author who would like to submit a non-fiction book proposal or a corporation that would like to have a book written for you. Please contact us by e-mail editorial@happyabout.info or phone (1-408-257-3000).

Other Happy About books available include:

- Blitz the Ladder
  http://happyabout.info/blitz.php
- Internet Your Way to a New Job
  http://happyabout.info/InternetYourWaytoaNewJob.php
- Happy About My Resume
  http://happyabout.info/myresume.php
- 30day BootCamp to Eliminate Fears & Phobias
  http://happyabout.info/30daybootcamp/fears-phobias.php
- DNA of the Young Entrepreneur
  http://happyabout.info/affiliates/dna.php
- I'm on Facebook–Now What???
  http://happyabout.info/facebook.php
- I'm on LinkedIn–Now What???
  http://happyabout.info/linkedinhelp.phpV
- Twitter Means Business
  http://happyabout.info/twitter/tweet2success.php
- They Made It!
  http://happyabout.info/theymadeit.php
- Happy About Online Networking
  http://happyabout.info/onlinenetworking.php

Dedication

To Mark (who knows all the ways to nurture an introvert!), Steph and Josh, for their unwavering love, appreciation, support, and encouragement

Acknowledgments

I want to thank the many people who were extremely generous with their time, sharing their experiences and observations about the trials and tribulations as well as the positive aspects of their introversion and/or shyness. Family, friends, colleagues, clients, and a number of strangers willingly and even eagerly made time for my questions. I am grateful to Mitchell Levy, publisher of Happy About, for giving me the opportunity to finally move forward with this book, and to the rest of the Happy About team, for the talent and skill they applied to the design, editing, and layout of the book.

I offer heartfelt gratitude and love to my family: to my parents—Doris, whose resilience, unsinkable spirit and insistence on making lemonade out of lemons will always inspire me, and Mickey, whose sensitive and empathetic essence lives on in the generations that follow; and to my sister Nancy, the consummate teacher, whose curious nature, positive outlook, and accepting manner helped me to find my own path.

Dive into the sea of thought, and find there pearls beyond price.

Moses Ibn Ezra

Contents

Introduction

My first encounter with the word "introvert" was in the fourth grade. I remember standing with my classmates around the desk of our teacher, Mrs. Nelson, while—for reasons I no longer recall—she explained to us the distinction between introverts and extraverts and suggested to each of us which one we were. She was quite explicit that neither was better or worse than the other, but when she told me I was an introvert, I was quietly disappointed. I didn't disagree. But I had already internalized the message from society that being outward-focused was the preferred style, despite her statement to the contrary.

Out of Sync

In our society, extraversion is often held up as the gold standard for all people to aspire to. As a result, the feeling of being out of sync is common among introverts. Because of the extraverted culture that we live and work in, we absorb a lot of negative messages that suggest we are somehow "less than" whatever is expected. People misinterpret our more reserved personalities—they think we're aloof, non-communicative, withholding, snobbish, and lots of other unflattering qualities. In my adulthood I was told that some of my extended family were concerned that there was something seriously wrong with me when I was little because I was so quiet.

Many of us recognize that we're out of sync with the rest of society and internalize the notion that there's "something wrong." Most of the images we see in the media are of people involved in extraverted activities. I remember being puzzled as a child by the exuberance shown by guests on quiz shows. I knew that even if I won the million-dollar jackpot, it simply would never be my style to jump up and down, scream with joy, and hug everyone around me. Sitcoms, dramas, reality shows—people are engaged in social activities. After all, how much drama is there in watching someone in a typically introverted activity such as reading or thinking?! There may be a lot of drama going on in that individual's head, but none of it is visible to the outside viewer. What's the fun in watching that? So there's little external recognition or validation of that behavior as something positive. Note—because there's been "so" much drama going on internally, the introvert may sometimes assume that all that activity "was" somehow apparent to the outside observer and be puzzled that coworkers or managers don't realize all that the introvert was engaged in.

With pressure all around us to be more extraverted, it's no surprise that this same message carries over into the professional realm, both on the job and in the job search. I came face-to-face with the typical extraverted advice in the job search world when I was entering my current profession as a resume writer/career advisor. Planning to put together a "tip sheet" on interview skills for my resume clients, I went to the library and found all the books I could on the subject (typical behavior for an introvert) and began to read through them. To my dismay, most of the books offered advice about horn tooting and sales and other behavior I couldn't relate to, which literally made me cringe and despair that "I could never do that." But I put my objections aside, thinking they were my own individual quirks and shortcomings, and adopted and even taught the commonly held views. (After all, all those experts can't be wrong, can they?) And then one day, as I was giving a workshop on interview skills, I came to a PowerPoint slide that said, "Sell yourself." Suddenly a hand went up, and a voice spoke out: "What are you supposed to do when you don't want to sound like you think you're the greatest thing since sliced bread?" As I looked around the room, I saw that about half the people in the room were nodding their heads in agreement. I suddenly realized this one individual had voiced the objections that are actually felt by many people but are often left unsaid. While some people hear that advice and feel empowered by it, others hear the same advice and feel diminished by it.

As I began to listen more to the objections and concerns of clients as they looked for new jobs and transitioned into them, I came to realize that there were few resources that addressed the issue of professional success from this perspective. My goal in writing this book is to pick up where other job search and career transition books leave off and to honor people of all types. If you've ever felt discouraged because you've heard that you have to "toot your own horn" or "sell yourself" or brag about all that you've done, rest assured that not everyone needs to play the horn to get a job or succeed in one. Employers, like orchestras, need a variety of instruments to create their music. It's possible to succeed without undergoing a personality makeover. This book will help you develop the skills and strategies that will enable you to present yourself so that an employer will understand and appreciate the unique "sound" that you will contribute to the organization.

At the same time, the purpose of this book is also to validate the experiences you've had as an introvert—quietly and often in isolation from others, perhaps not realizing that you share those experiences with many others and that you're not alone in your reactions to the world. Ultimately, I hope that you move from self-awareness to self-acceptance to self-appreciation, that you come to embrace and celebrate all that is positive about your introversion and to become comfortable in your own skin.

The biggest challenge in the job search process is that the skills required to be successful in the search are not the same skills required to be successful on the job. The search process requires a combination of strong social and communication skills, and the typical advice sends the message to introverts that they must transform themselves into extraverts in order to succeed. This book will look at the process from a different perspective—introverts can be successful by using their introverted strengths. In addition, introverts sometimes forget that there are disadvantages to being extraverted, as well, and I will speak to the fact that the grass isn't always greener on the other side. As Mrs. Nelson said, it isn't better or worse to be one or the other. The key is learning to capitalize on those situations where introversion gives us an advantage and to compensate for those where it puts us at a disadvantage.

Possibilities

A key theme throughout this book will be the notion of possibilities. Whether we are introverted or extraverted, shy or outgoing, we have choices and decisions about how we will behave in any situation. Both ends of the behavioral spectrum have advantages and disadvantages.

What's important is recognizing when introverted or shy behaviors serve our goals and when they interfere, so that we can select the behaviors that are most appropriate and effective for the task at hand. The key to success is versatility.

A lot of the standard advice on job search and career management comes in the form of "shoulds," such as "You've got to toot your own horn," "You have to sell yourself," and so on. This book is unusual in that it contains no shoulds. Instead, it contains suggestions that are intended to open up possibilities and provide choices. It recognizes that people are individuals and "one size does not fit all."

All of us make decisions based on our beliefs and assumptions about how the world works. But we don't always recognize when we're making assumptions, when our "beliefs" are really just stories that we've created to provide explanations for events when we have incomplete information about them. We introverts have such active inner worlds that we probably do that even more than the average person, and we don't even realize the extent to which we do it. Part of what I'll do in some of the strategies and suggestions I present is to provide what I call "reframes"—these are essentially alternative stories that you can use to replace the story you may be telling yourself if that story is holding you back from something you want or need to do. Since we base our behavior on stories, this approach allows you to pick stories that enable you to get where you want to go. Remember, too, that the stories that you have been telling yourself are not necessarily the stories that others are telling themselves—so your assumptions may be faulty in the first place.

In addition to the stories we tell ourselves, we also tell stories to others. These are the true stories you can share with employers in the course of your job search and with managers throughout your work life as a way to promote yourself. This book will provide a way to identify those stories and use them in your communications with prospective and actual employers.

Finally, another aspect of possibilities is the vast range of occupations that introverts choose and are successful in, from low-profile, behind-the-scenes jobs to positions of leadership and high visibility. Introversion is not a limiting characteristic, although the accompanying traits may require some special accommodations (also true of extraversion, but that's a subject for another book). We make comparisons to people who are highly successful and see the ways in which we fall short. Meanwhile, we don't get to see the struggles or challenges that they had to deal with, so their success looks falsely uncomplicated. We will look at stories of some famous people to apply some reality testing to our notions of what it means to be successful. Sometimes we only see the surface success and not the choices that lie beneath the success.

Introversion and Shyness

I've written this book for both introverted and shy people, although the two groups are not the same (Chapter 1 explains the distinction), as well as for people whose upbringing taught them more modest and reserved behavior, people who are uncomfortable promoting themselves. If you're introverted or shy, you typically dislike some of the heavily social aspects of the job search process—and there are many social aspects in the process—and as a result may feel at a disadvantage. You'll see throughout the chapters that follow that an effective job search also relies heavily on some of the skills we excel at and thrive on, and we actually have the edge in some parts of the process.

In those instances where success involves using other skills, I've tried to offer options for you to try, with the understanding that developing these other skills will enhance your effectiveness by adding to your other introverted strengths. I am not suggesting you need to be someone you're not. Note that, with regard to shyness, I sometimes refer to "overcoming" shyness because many people set that as a goal for themselves in response to their own internal discomfort; thus, I offer some strategies and quotes in support of that goal.

It's been fun to think about the population of introverts and shy people and to realize that one of the things that characterizes this group is that it isn't, in fact, a group. In the first place, most introverts and shy people, by definition, avoid groups. In a delightful paradox, one of my interviewees said, "We introverts have to stick together." I had to laugh at the imaginary "Professional Association of Introverts" organization that my mind conjured up as I thought about where to market this book. Who would attend the meetings?! In the second place, whether or not this population actually gathers together physically, the people within it are not all alike. There is a spectrum of behaviors, attitudes, values, and experiences. As a result, every strategy presented in this book will not work for each person who reads the book. Some of the strategies may even be contradictory. But all of them are offered because other introverts or shy people have found them helpful. You can select the ones that make sense to you, knowing that in one way or another they all take into consideration some of the attributes that make introverts distinct from extraverts.

The Writing Process

As an introvert, I tend to want to gather as much information as I can to make sure I really know what I'm talking about, to assure myself that I have a comprehensive understanding, before I offer my opinion. It's very easy to get distracted by any number of tangents and to want to dig deeper into each of those. It's hard to cut off the process and say that whatever information I have is enough. And this part of the process is much more fun for me than actually starting to formulate the language to express my findings.

Several aspects of this process required me to use my extraverted skills in order to move forward with this book. I had to begin to talk with people about my writing project, starting with a publisher, and present a compelling case for myself. Finding people to interview for my project was daunting. Mostly I relied on email, since I could reach more people with less expenditure of energy. Email also allowed me to avoid what may be my least favorite activity, making phone calls. In some instances, though, I needed to contact people by phone, including some strangers. This took me "way" out of my comfort zone. Most people were extraordinarily gracious as well as generous with their time and their observations. Everyone answered quite thoughtfully. Most people gave very comprehensive answers, clearly seeming to enjoy thinking about and chewing on these issues. A smaller number, having thought about the issues, synthesized their answers into much shorter answers that were very concise and to the point, and in some cases I experienced the reaction that I believe extraverts have, wishing people would elaborate and be less terse.

Interviewing people, contacting strangers, even just sharing with friends and colleagues that I was writing this book, all required me to manage my introversion and to apply several of the strategies I present in the book.

- "Eyes on the Prize" strategy (see Chapter 1) reminded me of my goal and its importance to me—getting this book written and published.

- "Feel the Fear and Do It Anyway" (see Chapter 4) helped me to approach many strangers. I emailed several people I discovered who blog on this topic—most responded positively and agreed to participate, but some didn't. I focused my energy on appreciating the generosity of those who offered to help and did not berate myself for "bothering" those who didn't respond. I gave myself alternative explanations for their lack of response and didn't dwell on it. For example, my email might not have reached them because of spam filters or because they simply deleted a message from a source they didn't recognize.

- "Reporting, Not Bragging" (see Chapters 3 and 5) came into play when people asked me, "What's new?" and I enthusiastically shared what I was working on. When I did so, to my surprise, many people revealed to me their own introversion or shyness and offered to share their experiences or provide help in any way they could. That hadn't been my intention in telling them what was going on with me. But I had given them specific information that they could then respond to. By defining myself and identifying my purpose, I had attracted the interest of others in ways I never imagined.

- On one occasion I became consumed with my own discomfort and tried all kinds of work-arounds to avoid doing something I thought I would be imposing on someone. When my work-arounds failed and I had to "impose," I discovered that my "imposition" had actually created an opportunity for someone else to track down information that was helpful to him, too—a reminder of the need to "Shift the Focus" (see Chapter 4).

In general, I had to manage energy flow throughout this project. There were parts of it that were very interactive, and I found that interviewing too many people in one day could be draining, so I tried to balance those interviews with the more inner-directed research and writing. I also found that I worked better if I could stay focused on a single task—and was thrown when, in a two-day span, I received three emails from my publisher urging me to come up with a subtitle for the book, select a cover design, and learn and use a new piece of software that would enable me to work collaboratively with my editor.

It's been interesting talking with so many introverts and seeing the range of behaviors. Some, predictably, asked to know my questions prior to actually talking, and some preferred to write out their answers rather than have a conversation. A few prepared specific answers to the questions I had given them and sounded uncomfortable with any follow-up questions that they hadn't had time to prepare for. But without exception, the answers I received from *everyone* contained a richness and depth that are breathtaking!

The people I interviewed for this book include family, friends, colleagues, and complete strangers. They range in age from mid 20s to mid 60s, with most in their 30s, 40s, or 50s and in the middle of their careers. They currently live in nine states in all regions of the country, and their past and present occupations cover a wide range of job titles, in both support and leadership roles. A partial list (in alphabetical order, with more than one person frequently represented in several of the categories) includes: administrative assistant, author, business development manager, career coach, college career services consultant, client relations manager, college professor, corporate writer, dental assistant, desktop publisher, director of corporate relations, doctor of osteopathy, documentation clerk, editor, EEO Affirmative Action manager, film director, financial services executive, fundraising researcher, healthcare researcher, human resources manager, Internet strategist and efficiency expert, life coach, MBA student/management consultant, mechanical engineer, medical researcher, organizational consultant, professional speaker, purchasing assistant, retail merchandiser, sales and customer service representative, social worker, software engineer, and teacher.

How to Use This Book

This will be the 20,000-foot view, not the in-depth treatment that, as an introvert, I was originally inclined to write. I decided that there is a lot of good information available about many aspects of job search, and I didn't want to repeat a lot of what's already been written about. Instead, I want to concentrate on those aspects of the process that are often sticking points for people who are introverted and shy, and to provide information specific to that population. In addition, I have included information on the newest trends in job search, many of which have not been written about in great detail for a wide audience.

The strategies presented here are intended to provide new options to try and to remove some of the discomfort from job search and career transition (recognizing that it's impossible to remove all of the discomfort). The purpose is to help you develop the versatility to apply skills that are appropriate to each situation, not to be someone you're not.

The book contains three sections. Section 1, "Foundations", explains in more detail the distinction between introversion and shyness and discusses the implications for job search. It also provides lists of famous people in both categories and presents some additional detail about the choices made by several successful celebrities. Section 2, "Job Search and Transition", looks at some of the traditional topics in a job search—finding job leads, creating an effective resume, interviewing, cultivating connections (networking), and successfully transitioning—but focuses on specific strategies geared toward those who are introverted or shy. Thus, we'll look at self-promotion, managing energy-draining social encounters, handling the spotlight, and thinking on your feet, as they come up again and again in the job search and on the job. The chapters in this section all follow the same format—they begin with a general introduction to the topic, followed by examples of typical stories that we tell ourselves that get in our way. Those are followed by a series of reframes of the stories, and then by specific strategies that you can choose from. These strategies come from a variety of sources: my own experience with introversion and shyness along with extensive research on shyness and introversion, the experiences of thousands of clients I've talked with over the years, and specific suggestions offered by numerous individuals who described themselves as introverted, shy, or both, and who generously shared their insights and observations with me specifically for this project. Finally, Section 3, "Embracing Your Introversion," recaps the strengths that introverts can be proud of and can draw on as they manage their professional lives. The book is designed so that you can read it in full, from start to finish, or you can just read the portions that address your specific concerns.

Section I
Foundations

1 Are You Introverted, or Are You Shy?

Shyness and Introversion: Not Identical

Most of us use the words shy and introverted interchangeably in everyday language, but they actually are different. While many people are both shy and introverted, some introverts are not shy, and some shy people are in fact extraverts. What shyness and introversion have in common is discomfort in social situations—in varying degrees and for different reasons. To an outside observer, shy and introverted behaviors often appear the same, although they may not be. Understanding the distinction is important in terms of identifying and developing strategies to manage job search and work life more effectively. Needless to say, both shyness and introversion comprise a spectrum of behaviors, and not all attributes apply to everyone. These are the most common.

Shyness—Shyness at its most basic is discomfort in the presence of others, characterized by self-consciousness. According to Dr. Signe Dayhoff, a social psychologist specializing in self-presentation, "shyness is a normal personality trait wherein there is inhibited behavior, a wariness of unfamiliar people, and timidity in situations which contain a risk of harm or failure."[1] Nearly 50% of the American population identify themselves as shy (a number that's increasing, according to researchers), with up to 95% saying they are or have been shy in some circumstances.[2] Safe to say that a job search is one of those circumstances!

If you've ever felt shy, you know the feeling. You fear being judged or criticized and typically dislike being in the spotlight. Common triggers of shyness include situations in which "a person can be observed and evaluated . . . this includes performing tasks, being tested, and speaking publicly, such as asking or answering questions, making comments, contributing to meetings, talking to authority figure, and making small talk."[3] In those moments, you're likely to be somewhat preoccupied with yourself ("I don't know what I should say, . . . do, . . . wear"). You may experience physical symptoms (racing heartbeat, sweating, blushing), difficulty concentrating, and a lot of negative self-talk. Throughout this book we will examine some of the negative stories we tell ourselves, do a reality check, and offer alternative and more empowering stories in the context of job search and career success.

Shyness comes in many forms. Perhaps you're among those who were shy at one time but have overcome your shyness. Or at the other end of the spectrum, you may be quite disabled by it. The good news about shyness is that, even if you can't change your shy feelings, you can change behavior or actions that are preventing you from reaching your goals. You have choices, and your shyness doesn't have to define or limit you. In some instances, shyness in mainstream American culture is seen as a negative and is sometimes equated with less competence and less intelligence. A couple of years ago I contacted a local organization to propose a workshop on networking for shy people and was told that the topic wouldn't attract people because it was "too negative." Other cultures view shy behavior differently. Swedes view shyness as a positive attribute, indicating sensitive, reflective, and non-pushy personalities.[4] In Japan, a well-known proverb states, "The nail that stands out is pounded down," resulting in

---

1. Signe A. Dayhoff, Ph.D., "How to Speak Without Fear Small Talk E-Course," http://speakwithoutfearnow.com/smalltalk-ecourse.htm, personal correspondence (email), July 10, 2008.
2. Bernardo J. Carducci, Ph.D., *A Bold New Approach*, Quill, 1999, p. 33.
3. Signe A. Dayhoff, Ph.D., "How to Speak Without Fear Small Talk E-Course," http://speakwithoutfearnow.com/smalltalk-ecourse.htm, personal correspondence (email), July 10, 2008.
4. Åke Daun, professor of ethnology at the University of Stockholm, *Ethnologia Scandinavica*, Vol. 28, 1998, "Describing a National Culture—Is it at all Possible?"

modest and reserved behaviors that decrease the likelihood of standing out.[5] Compare that with our saying, "The squeaky wheel gets the oil."

If you consider yourself shy (or if you have been at some point in your life), you're in good company. Look at the accompanying list, and you'll see that plenty of people whose careers place them in the limelight—such as entertainers, athletes, journalists, CEOs, and politicians—have struggled with shyness, along with others who have pursued less public occupations.

Famous Shy People[6]

Show Business
Julie Andrews • Kim Basinger • Carol Burnett • Jim Carrey • Johnny Carson • Tom Cruise • Kevin Costner • Robert De Niro • Bob Dylan • Sally Field • Ella Fitzgerald • Richard Gere • Whoopi Goldberg • Gene Hackman • Tom Hanks • Helen Hunt • Larry King • David Letterman • Mike Myers • Michelle Pfeiffer • Sidney Poitier • Elvis Presley • Julia Roberts • Carly Simon • Barbra Streisand • James Taylor • Barbara Walters • Denzel Washington • Sigourny Weaver • "Weird Al" Yankovic

History and Politics
Neil Armstrong • Rosalyn Carter • Thomas Edison • Albert Einstein • Al Gore • Thomas Jefferson • Abraham Lincoln • Pat Nixon • Rosa Parks • Eleanor Roosevelt • Bess Truman • Orville Wright

Literature/Art
Agatha Christie • T.S. Eliot • Lois Lowry • George Bernard Shaw • Charles Schultz • Harriet Beecher Stowe • Garry Trudeau • E.B. White

Business
Brenda Barnes • Michael Dell • Bill Gates • Katharine Graham • Kenneth D. Lewis

---

5. http://psychologytoday.com/articles/index.php?term=19951101–000030& page=6
6. The individuals listed have described themselves as shy or have been described as shy based on observation.

Journalism
David Brinkley • Peter Jennings • Jane Pauley • Frank Reynolds

Sports
David Beckham • Larry Bird • Roberto Clemente • Chris Evert • Mia Hamm • Marvin Harrison • Annika Sorenstam • Ricky Williams

Two celebrities, both of whom built their careers around interviewing people, have written about getting past their own shyness. Larry King, host of CNN's Larry King Live, wrote that the first rule of conversation is to listen, and noted that it helps to remember that whoever you're talking with is probably also shy.[7] ABC News journalist Barbara Walters wrote about the first time she was introduced to author Truman Capote, who had just published In Cold Blood. She was eager to ask him about it, but couldn't get past her own shyness and simply said, "How do you do," thinking he must be tired of talking about it.[8] That's the kind of negative self-talk that we all do from time to time, and in this case it stopped her from having the conversation she wanted. Her career since that time is proof that it's possible to make a different choice—and have a very different outcome.

Another famous American who transformed herself is former First Lady Eleanor Roosevelt. Shy and awkward as a child, she stepped into the spotlight to further her husband Franklin's political career when he was stricken with polio. She dedicated her life to advancing his political agenda and promoted many causes of her own. She expanded the role of First Lady, holding press conferences and giving lectures and radio broadcasts.[9] A champion of human rights, civil rights, and women's rights, she shifted her attention to serving others and chose not to let her shyness hold her back from the larger purpose[10]. By way of contrast, Eleanor's successor, Bess Truman, made a different choice in how she handled her role as First Lady. She disliked the pomp and pageantry of her role and preferred to stay out of the spotlight. She did only what she thought was absolutely necessary as First Lady.[11] Unlike her predecessor, she did not

---

7. Larry King, *How to Talk to Anyone, Anytime, Anywhere: The Secrets to Good Communication,* Crown Publishers, Inc., NY, 1994.
8. Barbara Walters, *How to Talk With Practically Anybody About Practically Anything,* Doubleday Co., Inc. Garden City, NY, 1970, p. xiii.
9. http://whitehouse.gov/history/firstladies/ar32.html
10. http://usinfo.state.gov/products/pubs/womeninfln/roosevelt.htm
11. http://whitehouse.gov/history/firstladies/et33.html

hold press conferences; she agreed to accept written questions, and she replied in writing, frequently with a "no comment."[12]

These stories illustrate the different choices that are possible for people who experience shyness. In the upcoming chapters, we'll talk about different strategies and choices for handling shyness when it presents itself in the job search process and in the transition to a new job.

Introversion—Introversion sometimes resembles shyness because many introverts are uncomfortable in social situations, but the source of that discomfort is very different. As originally described by psychologist Carl Jung, introverts find social encounters draining, particularly those involving a lot of people. Introverts gain energy from the inner world of ideas, and they typically enjoy periods of solitude to rejuvenate. Extraverts, by way of contrast, draw their energy from social encounters and find prolonged solitude draining.

Because introverts recharge their batteries by pulling away from social encounters, they are often labeled by others as shy. But not all introverts are, in fact, shy, and many do have good social skills. In fact, some introverts are quite outgoing, and many have shared with me the experience of being mistaken for extraverts—but they pay a price in terms of energy depletion. Those social encounters can be overstimulating, and introverts need to plan time to reenergize.

A second characteristic of introverts is that they process information more slowly than extraverts. The brains of introverts and extraverts use different pathways when processing information, and the introvert pathway is longer.[13] That explains why introverts speak of needing time to process information before they act or think, and describe encountering problems retrieving the word or thought that they're trying to think of. Some introverts report getting so caught up in the long pathway of their thoughts that they don't even realize they haven't communicated them out loud, or they start mid-thought, not realizing they haven't shared the early stages of their thoughts. As we'll see, energy depletion and information retrieval/communication issues become relevant in the context of job search activities and success on the job.

---

12. http://biography.com/search/article.do?id=9511096
13. Marti Olsen Laney, Psy.D., *The Introvert Advantage*, Workman Publishing, NY, 2002, pp. 74–75.

There are many assessments that can help identify whether someone is an introvert or extravert—the Myers-Briggs Type Indicator® instrument being among the most prominent, but you can get a quick idea which end of the spectrum you most likely fall on by asking yourself which of the following lists of attributes is generally the best fit, most of the time (keep in mind that these are not "all-or-nothing" characteristics, and most of us possess some degree of all of these, but most of us favor one group more than the other).

Introverts

Reflect before they talk or act

Are energized by solitude

Prefer socializing one-on-one to group events

Like periods of quiet; feel depleted after a lot of activity

Enjoy deep relationships with just a few select friends

Frequently turn their focus to thoughts, ideas, the inner world

Are characterized by depth of interest

Extraverts

Talk out loud as they think

Are energized by being around people

Enjoy large group activities

Like a lot of activities

Enjoy a wide circle of friendships

Frequently turn their focus to people, things, the outer world

Are characterized by breadth of interest

In psychological terms, having a "preference" for introversion or extraversion simply means that your energy more naturally flows in one direction or the other, inward or outward. It's a lot like being naturally right-handed (or left-handed). Assuming that you have the use of both hands, you can and do use your non-dominant hand in many activities, but it typically feels awkward to do so and more natural or comfortable to use your dominant hand. Most often, you use your non-dominant hand to support what your dominant hand is doing. As introverts, our dominant personality type draws us toward solitude and reflection or intimate conversations, and we learn to navigate in the outer world to balance our natural inclinations. As noted earlier, we're talking about a spectrum, and you'll find that there are situations where you may behave in more extraverted or introverted ways. Developing the versatility to apply whichever skills are most appropriate to the situation is one of the keys to success.

Unlike shyness, you can't "overcome" introversion; but like shyness, there are choices you can make that will enable you to manage it so that you can function most effectively in job search and work-related activities. And like shyness, you'll see that there are quite a number of famous and success-ful people who have been identified as introverts. Some, but not all, also appear on lists of shy celebrities.

Famous Introverts[14]

Show Business
Candace Bergen • Ingrid Bergman • Glenn Close • Michael Douglas • Clint Eastwood • Richard Gere • Katharine Hepburn • John Lennon • Sarah McLachlan • Shirley McLaine • Julia Roberts • Fred "Mister" Rogers • Steven Spielberg • Meryl Streep

History and Politics
Jimmy Carter • Calvin Coolidge • Diana, Princess of Wales • Thomas Edison • Albert Einstein • Dwight D. Eisenhower • Al Gore • Thomas Jefferson • Helen Keller • Abraham Lincoln • Jacqueline Kennedy Onassis • Eleanor Roosevelt • Bess Truman • Harry Truman

Business
Brenda Barnes • Warren Buffett • Henry Ford • Bill Gates • Katharine Graham • Charles Schwab

Journalism
Tom Brokaw • Peter Jennings • Diane Sawyer

---

14. Names on the list have been identified as probable introverts by numerous individuals, myself included, who are qualified to administer and interpret as-sessments such as the MBTI® instrument and are based on biographical infor-mation or observation.

Sports
Arthur Ashe • Ernie Banks • Bill Belichick • Bill Bradley • Michael Jordan • Roger Maris • Venus Williams

A few stories illustrate how some of these introverts managed their introversion as they pursued their careers and causes.

A *USA Today* article[15] described a number of corporate CEOs who have mastered extraverted skills but take time for solitude or quieter situations to recharge. They attribute some of their success to their inclination to think before they act.

Fred Rogers built a successful television show (Mister Rogers' Neighborhood), and a career, around his introverted qualities. Rejecting the animation and fast pace of many contemporary children's shows, Mister Rogers devoted each show to a theme—the in-depth approach favored by introverts. He spoke directly to the children in his audience, extending an invitation to his viewers that felt personal and intimate as he explored his neighborhood. In 1997, when he was awarded a Lifetime Achievement Emmy, he surprised the "glitterati" of the television world during his acceptance speech when he asked the audience for 10 seconds of silence to thank the people in their lives who helped them become successful. Ten seconds of silence in television is an eternity. But the audience complied, and people were moved to tears.[16]

Diana, Princess of Wales, applied her introverted need to pursue meaning in her life by taking her royal responsibilities to a deeper level. She expanded her role from simply visiting hospitals to championing larger causes and touching people (literally—contradicting royal protocol) who were suffering from diseases such as AIDS. She supported the International Campaign to Ban Landmines, winners of the Nobel Prize in 1997.[17]

Thomas Jefferson, both shy and introverted, was described by one biographer as someone who loved conversation but was unable to think on

---

15. http://usatoday.com/money/companies/management/2006–06–06-shy-ceo-usat_x.htm (http://tinyurl.com/p7px5)
16. http://technorati.com/videos/youtube.com/watch?v=X7-LkBE_CkM
17. http://biographyonline.net/people/diana/charity_work.html

his feet or speak extemporaneously,[18] a quality shared by many introverts. With strong beliefs about the nature and purpose of government, Jefferson fought for the causes he believed in through his writings, most famously the Declaration of Independence. As President, he delivered only two public speeches, at least in part because of his lack of eloquence.[19] He hosted private dinners and evening discussions/readings in philosophy and science in place of some of the customary large, formal events, state dinners, and presidential balls. After he left office, Jefferson, a quintessential man of ideas, continued to pursue his interests in areas such as architecture, astronomy, botany, animal husbandry, mechanical engineering, gardening, natural history, classical languages, and book collecting, and took great pride in founding the University of Virginia.[20]

These stories illustrate some of the ways that introverted qualities can contribute to success. The strategies noted below can help you manage shyness or introversion. The upcoming chapters will apply these and other strategies and choices to the process of job search and transition to a new job.

Strategies

Focus Outward—The very process of shifting your focus to others means you can't be self-conscious or focused on yourself. When you're serving others or attending to their needs or concerns, you'll be acting in ways that aren't shy.

Eyes on the Prize—This is closely related to the previous strategy, but rather than other people, the focus may be on a cause that's deeply important to you. This is the strategy Eleanor Roosevelt used in the earlier example.

Practice—All of the skills that you are trying to develop become easier with practice. Think of yourself as trying to improve the strength or agility in your non-dominant hand—it's awkward at first, but it becomes more natural as you do it more often. Model your behavior on those who have the skills you desire, and take small steps, changing one thing at a time. Remember that the goal isn't to change who you are but to increase your

18. Willard Sterne Randall—*Thomas Jefferson: A Life*, Henry Holt & Company, NYT, 1993, p. 17.
19. http://britannica.com/EBchecked/topic/302264/Thomas-Jefferson
20. http://millercenter.org/academic/americanpresident/jefferson/essays/biography/

versatility. (Note—two people I interviewed used the phrase "Fake it until you make it"—a curiously inauthentic-sounding phrase to my introverted ears. But when I asked for clarification, I was told that the authenticity comes from wanting to try on something new, to see who you can become, assuming you're uncomfortable in your shyness or want to become adept using your extraverted skills.) Practice also seems to help with information retrieval, which can be an issue for introverts.

Feel the Fear and Do It Anyway—Remember that your feelings may not change, but your behavior can. And sometimes, with practice, the feelings actually "may" change. The focal point isn't the feeling, it's the action.

Reject Rejection—Sometimes shyness stems from fear of rejection. Remind yourself that there are many explanations for people saying "no" and many of those rejections have nothing to do with you.

Manage Energy Flow—Recognize which activities are draining and plan your schedule accordingly. Inform others of your need to recharge your batteries, so they won't misunderstand your removing yourself from the group.

Value Yourself—Remember that it's neither good nor bad to be an introvert or an extravert. It simply is. Appreciate the strengths and compensate for the weaknesses that come with your style, and set reasonable goals for yourself.

Quotes

Shyness

Susan Whitcomb, author and career coach

"I started to view my shyness as a selfish behavior. In other words, I was more concerned about what others thought of me than what others might need. That was the biggest turnaround for me to move out of my shyness."

"I'm also more aware that people might perceive me as aloof or stuck up if I don't reach out, and I do NOT want that perception of me (it's not an accurate one), so that helps me to reach out more. On some occasions, I am able to use my extraverted colleague to help with this as well. She can help make the initial contact and then introduce the person to me."

Deb Dib, CEO career strategist, http://ExecutivePowerBrand.com

"For me, managing shyness, what was most helpful was 'fake it till you make it.' Just do it, just putting everything toward people and not towards yourself, going from that service perspective. The biggest thing is having something that I want to say that I know is going to help somebody. The adrenaline of wanting to have that message that's going to help someone pushes the fear down."

Barbie Dallmann, certified Professional Life Coach, http://CoachBarbie.com

"Feel the fear and do it anyway. Pretend you're not [shy]. Fake it till you make it. How would a not-shy person act."

From Kate Duttro, career consultant/coach and college career counselor

"Both parents were quite shy, quiet people . . . I didn't have a role model for 'social assertiveness.' Worked through it through 'exposure to the larger world.' Once I realized that, I was able to pay more attention to people who did have good social skills."

Meghan Wier, business writer/author: *Confessions of an Introvert, The Shy Girl's Guide to Career, Networking and Getting the Most Out of Life*

[work through shyness] "I think that it just takes being exposed to situations over and over again to gain a comfort level, and lose some shyness."

"Marcia," career development facilitator

"So I think I worked through any shyness by making friends, and finding success and attention in certain endeavors. I wanted to be known as someone who is smart and talented, and not to be defined by pejorative labels like 'shy.'"

Ann Lawthers, senior director, evaluation and measurement

"When I was in graduate school for my doctorate, I made a conscious effort to say something at least once every class session. I had discovered by then that I did have good thoughts and if I didn't express those thoughts someone else would, so I might as well try to be first. Later, in meetings, I applied the same principle—one comment per meeting."

"Douglas," formerly mechanical engineer, now MBA student/ management consultant

"I worked through [shyness] using a variety of strategies: (1) 'Confidence due to general indifference:' You can't care how people react to you, and realize that, if an interaction goes badly, chances are you're never going to see that person again. I used to be very concerned about how I was perceived in social situations, and this is a big issue in networking at b-school. I had to realize that, in fact, I wouldn't see most people I interact with again if it doesn't go well. And I had to learn to be OK with that. (2) 'Low-stress, low value:' I would literally find people to talk with in every-day life to try and teach myself not to be anxious making small talk with people. If I were to 'screw up' talking to any one of these people, it would have virtually no negative impact on my life."

Dean Lincoln Hyers, film director / professional speaker

"Feel the fear and doing it anyway. Fear is okay. You might as well embrace it because you can't get away from it. I'm not over my fears. I'm over running from my fears."

Patty Lebau, teacher

"I might feel awkward, I might feel shy, I might feel embarrassed, I might even feel there's a sense of judgment, but I make a conscious decision not to react to that. I don't have to react to those things. If I want to do something, such as interact with someone, I don't have to allow my first response to govern the situation."

Dianne, dental assistant, medical researcher

"I became very aware of it [shyness] and I forced myself; forced the issue . . . being shy just wasn't gonna work."

Dr. Terrie Wurzbacher, author of *Your Doctor Said What?*

"I think of myself as shy, but one of the painful things for me is I like to be around people. I can be by myself now, but I really like people and want to get to know them and interact with them but I can't, something is holding me back. Two books, The Four Agreements and The Aladdin Factor, have made the biggest difference in my life in being able to talk to people, knowing that if they're saying no, they're not necessarily saying no to me. . . . Most of my shyness is a fear of rejection."

Rick Sullivan, director of software engineering, GateRocket, Inc.

"I found this [meeting and interacting with people at work that I don't know] quite stressful in my early career; but such meetings and interactions are now so common, I wonder how I could have been shy about this early on. I think the mechanism I used to work through it is 'repeated exposure'; doing it over and over again, so it becomes second nature."

Signe A. Dayhoff, Ph.D., *How to Speak Without Fear Small Talk E-Course*, http://speakwithoutfearnow.com/smalltalk-ecourse.htm

"Whenever you have negative thoughts or feelings about a social situation that arouse fear, make a point to examine them and check to see if they reflect the reality of the situation. Specifically, you need to look for concrete specific evidence in the situation to support them. When you don't find it, dispute each irrational thought with facts—why it isn't so. Also employ abdominal breathing to reduce physiological arousal because when you don't feel physically fearful, it's hard to think fearfully."

Introversion

Meghan Wier, business writer/author: *Confessions of an Introvert, The Shy Girl's Guide to Career, Networking and Getting the Most Out of Life*

"Take time for yourself—every day. Make that part of your routine, if it is going to the gym, an afternoon nap, reading a book, or taking a walk—but time alone is VERY important."

Ann Lawthers, senior director, evaluation and measurement

"Listen to yourself. When you feel that you have been with people too long, go hide in your office. If you live in cube land—go outside your building. Let others in on your 'secret.' Explain that it is about energy. Practice the appearance of extraversion. Do little 'tests' of the water and see how it makes you feel and expand the number and length of tests gradually."

Dianne, dental assistant, medical researcher

"I need my space. I need my own space to rekindle the fires and refresh myself. . . .I would go for a walk; I walk a lot. Or go into the woods and sit on a rock or something."

Jeanne Knight, career and job search coach

"I think it's important for introverts to recognize that every once in a while they are going to have to behave outside of their comfort zone . . . either to be successful at work or in their job search, or to create strong connections with people in a social situation. The key is to recognize that, do it, and then make sure you set aside enough time for rest and rejuvenation. Knowing that you've set aside the time for rejuvenation can make the times when you have to act 'extraverted' a little easier to swallow."

"Sandy," corporate writing trainer

"Our world operates better for extroverts; if you find yourself not operating well in that environment, you can say, well, I just don't have the goods, or you can say I have the goods that meet a different situation."

**Barbie Dallman, certified Professional Life Coach,
http://CoachBarbie.com**

"Not placing a value judgment on whether that's good or bad. It is what it is. It's just who you are. It uniquely qualifies you for a variety of tasks, things that you can do very well because that's who you are. Accepting that and loving that—when you start out thinking it's flaw, that's what you communicate, rather than this is a gift that I bring."

Nancy Loderick, Internet strategist and efficiency expert

"I think it's most important not to beat myself up [about the things I didn't get done]."

**Dean Lincoln Hyers, film director / professional speaker,
http://sagepresence.com**

"The cool thing about being introverted or shy, you will experience every piece of progress in such a deep and rich way that you will get an enjoyment that is big enough that will trump the things that are holding you back. Introverts have a capacity for depth that allows them to have rich and vibrant success even if they take only 1 step instead of 50. The extrovert has to take the 50 steps, working harder to feel the depth. The introvert doesn't have to work as hard.

Section II
Job Search and Transition

2 | Finding Job Leads

Being introverted or shy poses special challenges in the job search process, with its heavy emphasis on social skills. The following chapters will highlight those aspects of the process that draw on the strengths of introverts while also suggesting strategies that can be helpful in those stages that tend to be challenging. We'll begin by looking at what you can do to identify job opportunities.

Since the mid-1990s, the Internet has increasingly become a part of the job search process. People who are shy or introverted, in particular, have taken full advantage of the opportunity to post their resume and conduct much of their search by responding to online postings. Generally speaking, this strategy works best when combined with others, which will be outlined below.

Change the Story

We tell ourselves a lot of stories that get in our way. For example:

"Searching online is the most important job search strategy. If I concentrate my energies on posting my resume online and then diligently scour the various job sites and send out resumes to every appropriate opportunity, I'm doing all I need to do to find a job."

"I don't care what kind of job I get—I'll take anything."

The rest of this chapter will discuss reframes of those stories and will present strategies to help you maximize your results.

Multiple Paths

Figuring out where the job opportunities are is a big part of the challenge of the job search process, and whether you're an introvert and or an extravert, you will be drawn toward the path of least resistance. That path will lead you to jobs that are advertised in various places, such as newspapers, Internet job boards, and postings at college and state career services offices. It's also a particularly comfortable path for those who are introverted or shy, because uncovering these opportunities falls into the category of research, a nice, solitary activity that is usually well within our comfort zone. So a caveat, especially to introverts: remember to balance your introverted activities with some extraverted ones to achieve the best results.

The other path to explore will typically require more effort, but it will take you to the land of the so-called "hidden job market," or unadvertised jobs, where you'll be able to uncover the very sizable number of job opportunities that are not posted. Studies have shown that anywhere between two-thirds and three-quarters of all jobs may fall into this category! Many of the traditional activities required to tap into these possibilities are more extraverted activities, but this chapter will present strategies you can use that draw on your introverted strengths. In fact, you'll find that there are some aspects of this process in which introverts probably have something of an advantage over extraverts.

It's a good idea for you to explore both the advertised and the unadvertised paths for a shorter and more productive job search. It's also helpful to track your activities as you go along. How much time are you spending on different activities? If you get stuck in a pattern of little return on your investment of time, change the proportion of time you're spending in each area to see if that produces different results. And make sure you are, in fact, exploring all the possible avenues. Tracking your activities will also reassure yourself (and your loved ones, whose well-intentioned impatience can sometimes add to the pressure you're already feeling) that you are doing all that you can do.

Focus Your Search

Sometimes people say they don't care what they do, they just need a job. They think that, if they cast a wide net, they are more likely to land something. You'll find that the opposite is true—that the more you narrow what you're looking for, the easier it is to find—and to receive useful help from other people once they understand what it is that you're looking for.

Strategies

Advertised Jobs

Newspaper Ads—Many employers still place ads in newspapers, particularly smaller organizations and those that are looking to draw from a narrow geographic area. However, newspaper classified sections are growing smaller, so don't rely only on them. And understand that the ads that are printed in the written publication are not always the same ads that are posted on the newspaper's Web site, so be sure to check both places.

Internet Job Sites—These have entered the job search landscape in a big way in the past decade, and they allow you to apply to a lot of jobs very easily—and very introvertedly. Among the better-known job sites, as of this writing, are http://careerbuilder.com, http://monster.com, http://hotjobs.yahoo.com/, and http://craigslist.org/, with http://idealist.org being well-recognized for nonprofit jobs and http://usajobs.gov for federal government jobs. Another site to explore is called http://indeed.com, which is a search engine that searches other job boards, company Web sites, professional association sites, and other relevant sites to identify jobs that match the criteria you select. A similar site, http://simplyhired.com, also links to the http://linkedin.com networking site, which is discussed below in Web Identity. You can learn about industry-specific sites at http://weddles.com.

Company Web Sites—Placing ads in newspapers or on job boards costs companies money, and when the economy is flooded with people seeking work, companies sometimes choose not to place ads in newspapers or on job boards and to advertise only on their own site. They are looking to hire people who want to work specifically for them, not just people who want "a job." If you are interested in that company, they figure, you'll visit their site directly to find out the company's hiring needs. A good strategy in any job search is to develop a list of target companies or organizations that you would like to work for and that can use your unique combination of skills, credentials, and personal attributes, and to look for openings at those companies. As you'll see shortly, this strategy crosses over into the Unadvertised Opportunities section, as well.

Recruiters/Staffing Companies (Pros and Cons)—The Pros: The ideal circumstance for an introvert is to have someone else promote you. Recruiters and staffing companies can serve that purpose, connecting you with jobs that you qualify for. In particular, staffing companies can connect you with temporary or temp-to-perm opportunities, which are increasingly becoming an avenue that employers use to "hedge their bets" before bringing a candidate on board permanently. Temp and contract opportunities exist in all fields and at all levels. You can find links to recruiting firms through the Riley Guide: http://rileyguide.com/recruiters.html. The American Staffing Association lists staffing companies: http://ameri canstaffing.net/jobseekers/find_company.cfm   (http://tinyurl.com/4f35c2). Kennedy Information publishes a list of executive recruiters: http://kennedyinfo.com/js/der.html. The Cons: However, keep in mind that recruiters don't actually work for you—that is, they are paid by companies to fill positions. If you match the specifications they're looking for, they'll be interested in helping you because they stand to earn a nice commission if they place you. But the employer pays the commission. If you're not a good fit, they don't get paid to try to uncover possibilities that do match. They don't perform the role of an agent, where you pay them to present and represent you in the hiring transaction (as much as we wish someone would do that for us).

Professional Association Web Sites—Some professional association sites post relevant job openings. Worth checking. And again, there's an opportunity for "unadvertised" job search through professional associations, as we'll see below. You can find a comprehensive list of professional associations at http://weddles.com.

Job Fairs—Job fairs can be a useful place to connect one-on-one with employers. You can find local job fairs through your state one-stop career centers (http://servicelocator.org/) and on many of the Internet job boards noted above. Usually the job fair announcements will link to the employers in attendance, so you can check to see if there are jobs that you qualify for and seek out those specific employers—that will enable you to manage your energy at these large gatherings and to seek out the most promising opportunities. If energy and time permit, consider one or two stops to talk with employers that are of lesser interest to you for an opportunity to practice your interviewing and other interpersonal skills where there's less at stake. Then move on to the employers that most interest you.

Unadvertised Opportunities

Target Companies—This strategy builds on the process we've just discussed, to develop a list of companies that you'd like to work for and looking on the company Web sites for appropriate positions. However, I encourage you to take this process a step further. It's entirely possible that there will be no suitable openings at the time you begin your search. So another step is to look for opportunities to talk with people who work there now or who worked there previously. Do some information gathering. What's it like to work for that company? What are its current challenges? What's happening with the competition? How might someone with your skills fit in? Here's where you can apply your inclination to "go deep" and really get to know about the organization. The sources of this information, the people who work(ed) there, can be found simply by asking your current contacts if they know people at your target companies who might be willing to have a conversation with you. This is all done at a one-on-one level, first with people you already have relationships with and who are inclined to want to help with your job search, and then with their contacts. It's been my experience writing this book that even strangers are willing to take time to provide information and advice if they think they can be helpful. In addition, business networking sites such as http://linkedin.com can enable you to locate and connect with people at target companies (additional information and advice will be presented on this topic in the Chapter 4). Caveat: Watch out for spending too much time doing research and not enough time actually applying for jobs or networking or engaging in other activities that will ultimately bear fruit.

Web Identity—Look for forums and other opportunities to exchange ideas with people in your industry. As an introvert, you can enjoy the opportunity to reflect on what you want to say before you post your thoughts, but at the same time you are interacting with others and making yourself professionally visible. You can post questions or provide answers and establish your professional expertise. Increasingly, recruiters are using the Internet to find professional talent. In addition to participating in professional discussions, check to see what recruiters will find when they "Google" your name—will they find you at all, and if so, will it be in a professionally positive light. Besides professional forums, there are many ways to create a Web identity for yourself. For example, you can develop a professional blog in your area of expertise. Discuss the latest trends in your field, review presentations or books you've heard or read, present your own research findings, and so on. You can also create a Web portfolio, using audio and video, links to other sources, and other tools to showcase your achievements in more detail. In addition, you can create a profile on professional networking sites such as LinkedIn or Facebook, and invite your contacts to participate. This is an easy way to capitalize on the one-on-one relationships that introverts prefer. LinkedIn has a question-and-answer board that provides a place to help others while at the same time positioning yourself as knowledgeable in your field. This tool plays to the strengths of introverts by giving you time to reflect on the questions and carefully think through your answers. Employers also look at these sites to find promising candidates, so remember that whatever pictures or information you put out there need to reflect a positive and professional image.

Quotes

Jason Alba, CEO, JibberJobber.com, author of *I'm On LinkedIn: Now What?* and *I'm On Facebook: Now What?*

"Social networking sites allow you to get to know others in the comfort of your own home, with some level of being anonymous. Even though you are saying who you are, and they are saying who they are, we still get time to digest their message and personality, and determine if this is someone we want to forge a relationship with. Instead of the other person being 'in my face,' I can move forward at a pace that I'm comfortable with."

"Interestingly enough, some of the people I know who are more 'aggressive' on social networks like LinkedIn and Facebook are quiet and reserved in a face-to-face environment!"

Donna Jean Kaiser, mechanical engineer

"Keep a log of activities—so you can see your progress, or lack of, and have something to analyze; be objective about your progress (because you can so easily lose perspective)."

Kathy Scarpone, administrative specialist

"I found temping to be helpful while looking for a permanent job—and often times, finding permanency through temping. It worked out perfectly, because I already knew the culture, the people, the job and made it more than it was first written up to be."

Patty Lebau, teacher

"[Job search] has always been a not-fun process, but when I changed it into a research project, I was able to turn it into something I could handle. A research project is the kind of intellectual area that I'm comfortable with."

3 Promoting Yourself

Creating an Effective Resume

If you're like most people—introverts and extraverts alike—you're probably about as eager to write your resume as you are to undergo root canal. In addition to the challenges of finding the right words and phrases and formatting the document so that it is attractive, you have to deal with strategic questions about what information to include and with the emotional discomfort of appearing boastful.

Entire books have been written that describe the first two aspects of resume writing, the mechanics and strategy of writing, and formatting a resume that will open doors. I won't attempt to reinvent that wheel here, although I'll touch on some of the key elements. Instead, this chapter will pick up where many of those books leave off, by focusing on the content of the resume—determining what information to put on the resume in the first place, particularly in the context of the discomfort that introverted or shy people feel when it comes to promoting ourselves.

Change the Story

We tell ourselves a lot of stories that get in our way. For example:

"Resumes are full of deception and exaggeration."

"I didn't do anything distinctive or unique. I just did my job."

"I don't want to sound like I'm bragging."

"Who am I to be talking about what I've done?"

The rest of this chapter will discuss reframes of those stories and will present strategies to help you find compelling content for your resume.

Accentuate the Positive

It's a misconception that resumes have to be filled with exaggeration and hyperbole. Resumes do not need hype or embellishment in order to be effective. In fact, hype and embellishment can actually be counterproductive. Rather, effective resumes use strategic inclusion and placement of information as the primary method to accomplish their objective, which is to get you an interview. A good resume is like flattering clothing—some styles highlight your best features, while others call attention to the features you don't want noticed. A well-designed and well-written resume does the same thing—it accentuates the positive, highlights your strengths, and makes a good first impression. Most of us feel good in clothing that makes us look good; your resume can make you feel good, too, as it makes you look your most attractive to a prospective employer.

Ask Not What the Company Can Do for You

Remember President Kennedy's inaugural quote? "Ask not what your country can do for you. Ask what you can do for your country." An effective resume answers the question, "What can you do for the company?" Your communication with prospective employers in the early stages of the process will emphasize how you can be an asset to the organization; it will not focus on your questions about salary, benefits, or the other tangibles that the company will give to you.

Employers want to hire people with specific skills, credentials, and personal attributes that will solve a particular problem that their organization faces. A strong resume demonstrates the match between your background and experiences and the needs of the employer. Job postings can help you uncover those needs—see what requirements are listed, and make sure your resume (and cover letter) mentions the specific ways that you meet those requirements.

Essentially, the resume will tell the story of what you've done in your various jobs. It needs to highlight what distinguishes you from others who have held similar jobs, so the employer can get a clear picture of what it's like to have you as an employee. The emphasis is on *you*, not on the job you held. If your resume contains statements that could appear on the resumes of others with your job title, those statements are too generic. (A typical generic—and ineffective—teacher resume might contain a sentence that says, "Planned and taught lessons in language arts, math, science, and social studies." That statement describes almost all elementary school teachers. A better, specific statement would be something like, "Introduced an integrated unit on trees in which students 'adopted' trees in a local park, studied the changes over time (science), estimated the number of leaves (math), and wrote poems about them (language arts)." This story illustrates what it's like to have this teacher in charge of a class. It involves no deception, no embellishment. It simply tells a true story. Or compare the generic statement for an administrative assistant: "Created Excel spreadsheets." with the specific story: "Developed color-coded Excel spreadsheet to track and coordinate monthly schedules of 15 staff." These examples demonstrate that even people who do the same job don't do it the same way.

Remember, too, that once we learn our jobs well, they seem very easy to us, and we have a tendency to downplay the skills that we've developed and the accomplishments we've achieved. "No big deal. Anyone would have done that." Not true. Only someone with your specific skills, experience, judgment, and so on would have done that. Or done it that exact way. We are not interchangeable cogs. The more you can define what distinguishes you from others, the better you can communicate what you have to offer to employers.

"Reporting," Not "Bragging"

You may be thinking that detailing your accomplishments or telling these stories is being boastful. Perhaps you come from a culture where it's considered unacceptable to promote yourself in this manner. Or you don't want to appear to take full credit for what was a team effort. If all you're doing is reporting facts, that's not bragging. You're telling a series of stories that describe events at work—problems you encountered, actions you took, and results you achieved. You're simply providing information about things that occurred. Focusing on storytelling, using a problem–action–result (P-A-R) format, is a good way to convey to an employer the kinds of contributions you can make. For example, your story might say, "In an economic downturn, developed new merchandising strategy that increased customer traffic and produced a 10% increase in sales." You've described the problem (the difficult economy), your action (developed new merchandising strategy), and the result (increased customer traffic and produced a 10% increase in sales). Your stories can indicate if you accomplished something as an individual or as a member of a team. Again, there's no misrepresentation of the facts, and the employer can ask for more details in an interview to find out your specific role. In addition, you can include feedback from others in your resume—you're simply reporting what they said (see "Just the Facts" later in this chapter).

Completing the Puzzle

Once you've identified the stories you want to tell, ask yourself, "If employers learn only five things about me, what are the most important five things for them to know." Pick the stories that illustrate those points, and present those first, ideally in the top third or half of the page. You can find examples of different formats and styles in the many resume books on the market to see how you might do that. Remember that most employers only glance at your resume, usually spending no more than 30 seconds in the initial scan. If you don't hook them immediately, they may not read the entire document. In addition, medium to large size companies generally use computers to scan the resumes for keywords that are important to them, so be sure that you go through a number of job postings for your position to see what employers might be looking for, and then include those words in your document.

Keep in mind two general rules about resumes. The first is that they must be honest and accurate. Honest means no exaggerations, and certainly no lies. Accurate means they are factually correct and free of typos and grammatical mistakes. (My favorite typo was when the intended phrase "assisted clients" appeared as "assassinated clients"—not many employers are looking to hire people with that skill!) The second general rule: The rest is strategy. What you include, what you omit, where you position things on the page, all will be determined by thinking about the employer's needs—what you can do for the company—and telling stories that indicate your ability to meet those needs.

Strategies

Just the Facts—Present the facts, just the facts, not embellishments or exaggerations, in order to present your most flattering attributes. You can be selective with regard to which information you reveal—the resume isn't a complete autobiography, and you get to choose the information that portrays you at your best.

Show and Tell—Create a portfolio with samples of your work (e.g., charts, reports, newspaper articles, certificates, documents you created, performance reviews, testimonials). Your portfolio will provide you with material for your resume. You can also bring it with you to the interview and use it to generate or support points for discussion. Moreover, you can create a Web portfolio with links to the various items.

Testimonials—Gather performance reviews, testimonials, quotes, letters of thanks or praise, etc.—list the tasks people acknowledged and the skills or attributes they praised. Create "recognized for…" or "recognized as…" statements. These add credibility when the praise comes from others. In addition, allowing yourself to fully process the compliments will add to your ability to believe in and communicate your value to the employer, both on paper and in an interview.

Tower of Strength—Build a list of strengths or accomplishments. Ask friends or coworkers to help you identify content for your resume. "Everyone" can identify with the difficulty of writing a resume. You can say to someone, "I'm trying to put together a resume. That's always such a challenge, because I feel like I'm bragging. I wonder if you could help me out by sharing a few of the things that you thought I did well when we worked together."

Before and After—Compare your job as you found it when you were first hired with your job now (or when you left it). How did things change? What was your role in the change?

Passion—Describe aspects of your work that you most enjoy or when you lose all sense of time. The activities that excite you are the ones that you will talk about with the most energy, ease, and animation. By including them on your resume, you invite the interviewer toward the topics that you can talk most comfortably and enthusiastically about.

Quotes

Claire, social worker

"Outplacement had me go through each of my jobs and list three things that I felt really good about. I realized I really did accomplish some things. It was a reframe that it wasn't tooting my own horn as much as just stating, factually, here are some things that I've done."

Wayne Purnell, organizational consulting

"A lot of people think of that as bragging, so if they can frame it in a different way, accentuating the positive—some things won't speak for themselves, you need to highlight them."

Donna Jean Kaiser, mechanical engineer

"It was helpful to go over old annual reviews—made me feel better—and helped me summarize accomplishments in a positive way."

4 Cultivating Connections

This is the obligatory chapter about networking. I avoided using the word in the chapter title, because the term is toxic to so many people. Probably more than any other activity, networking pulls you out of your comfort zone if you're shy or introverted. (It sparked the most commentary and suggestions from interviewees.) The paradox is that the essence of networking is building relationships, something that many introverts actually excel at—when those relationships are one-on-one. Networking is a key ingredient in finding a job and in managing your career, but there are many ways to do it. If you think of it in terms of cultivating connections, developing long-term, ongoing relationships, the process will feel less superficial and more genuine, which is networking at its best—and introverts at their best.

Change the Story

We tell ourselves a lot of stories that get in our way. For example:

"I'm afraid I'd be imposing; I don't want to bother people or be a burden."

"How can I call someone I don't know or I've lost touch with? It feels like I'm using people."

"People are too important or too busy to talk to me."

"I can't stand the superficiality of small talk; can't stand large gatherings."

"I never know what to say; I'm no good at working the room."

"I can do this on my own. I don't need help."

"I feel like I'm asking for charity."

"If I don't come away with a job lead, it's a waste of my time."

The rest of this chapter will discuss reframes of those stories and will present strategies to help you find opportunities to comfortably cultivate relationships as both a job search and career management activity.

Giving and Getting

Part of the discomfort with networking is that it seems self-serving. Phrases like "work the room" have unfortunately entered the lexicon, and they suggest a kind of activity that is highly distasteful to people who are looking for in-depth relationships. In reality, networking is a mutual process—if you focus your attention on listening to learn what the other person's needs are, you take some of the uneasiness out of the picture. Listening is one of the skills introverts excel at, so concentrate on finding out what's important to those you network with, and be generous and sincere in offering information and help. A mutual exchange is at the core of all relationships, and when you place your attention on serving others or learning from others, you will find this process both more interesting and less daunting.

Wired to Help

Networking at its most basic is simply sharing information and resources for mutual benefit. We do that all the time outside of the context of job search and career—ask for the name of a good mechanic, give advice on gardening, alert friends to a new book or movie or restaurant that we know will interest them, and so on. Yet for some reason our stories get us tangled up when a job or career enters the picture.

It helps to turn the situation around and imagine yourself being on the receiving end of a phone call or an inquiry from somebody you know (or who knows a contact of yours), asking for some advice. I've asked this question to hundreds of people in the workshops I give, and with "no" exceptions, they all say they would be happy to help if the situation were reversed. As human beings, we're programmed to help others, even total strangers. Think about any of the catastrophic events that are reported on the news. The stories always provide information on where people can donate money or food or clothes or whatever is needed. And people always come through. The process breaks down when we don't know what to do to help. Figuring out and communicating specifically what kind of assistance you need is the key to tapping into people's natural inclination to help. And keep in mind, as you think about how others can be helpful to you, that you want to also be listening to how you can be helpful to them.

Be prepared to provide and to seek information in the following ways (some of these are specific to job search; some are appropriate both in job search and general career management):

- Provide the name of somebody to talk to in the industry or in a particular company

- Offer resume feedback

- Share information, articles, links on new trends in the industry

- Provide answers to questions in your (or their) area of expertise

- Identify/suggest job titles in a new field; offer advice on transferring from a former career into a new career you're exploring

- Pass a resume along to a hiring manager

- Provide specific company information

- Explain "how did you get started in your field?"

- "Catch up" and exchange information casually

Seek "Advice"

If you struggle with the idea of asking for "help," think about asking for "advice" instead. You'll find people more than eager to give advice—

sometimes even when we *don't* ask for it! Asking for advice focuses the conversation on the information needed and maintains the balance of the relationship. In addition, the people you approach are likely to feel flattered that you respected their opinion and sought their advice, so you're actually making them feel good.

Planting Seeds

Think of networking as planting seeds. You don't know which ones are going to sprout or when, but eventually some do. The more seeds you plant, the more will take root. This process is nonlinear, indirect, and serendipitous. It's also long term and multi-step. It can be hard to be patient with the process when you want or need immediate results, but if you approach your networking activities with a mindset that is long term and open to possibilities, you may be pleasantly surprised. As with any relationships, if you enter them not attached to the outcome, not invested in a specific result, you are more likely to have a positive outcome of some sort.

Rejection Raincoat

A client once shared with me the technique that she was taught as part of her sales training, which allowed her to not take rejection personally. She imagined putting on a rejection raincoat prior to making cold calls. Anytime someone said "no," the "no" just rolled off the raincoat and didn't touch her. The key is remembering that it's not about you if someone does say no. The person might be having a bad day, or you may have caught them at an inconvenient time, or they might not have understood what you were asking. If they didn't return a message, perhaps there was a mechanical or electronic malfunction or a filter or gatekeeper and your message didn't actually get through. You did nothing wrong by reaching out to them. Provide yourself with a story that keeps your ego intact.

Another story that can be helpful is to recognize that certain people you might like to approach already aren't helping. You have nothing to lose and everything to gain if you ask. If they say no, you're right where you started. If they say yes, you're ahead of the game. My experience writing this book involved reaching out to a lot of strangers (and applying many of the techniques in this chapter to change my own unhelpful stories as I prepared to call on people in the first place and then had to deal with the occasional "no" response), and I found most people incredibly gracious and obliging.

In addition, the people who already knew me were fully supportive and helpful in ways that I couldn't have anticipated. When it comes to contacting people you've lost touch with, remember that the responsibility for staying in touch wasn't entirely yours—most likely people will be delighted to hear from you and glad to help if they can. When I've asked in workshops if people would welcome a call from a voice from the past, even if the person was calling in a moment of need, again it's been unanimous—people are glad to reconnect.

Inclusion vs. Isolation

My mother taught me that allowing someone else to help is actually a gift you give to them—it gives them the gratification of helping others and the opportunity to do something meaningful. There's no honor or higher moral integrity in missing out on an opportunity because you chose to stand alone. My husband, Mark, once submitted a resume in response to an Internet posting—it was one of those "perfect fit" jobs—but surprisingly got no reply. When a former manager learned that Mark had applied to that particular company, he mentioned the name of a contact he had there. Mark called the contact and was immediately invited to meet with the hiring team, who happened to be in town and had just finished interviewing the candidates they had selected—Mark obviously had not been among them. A week later, after this spur-of-the-moment interview, he received two letters on the same day: a form letter rejecting him (in response to his Internet application), and a letter offering him the job (in response to his interview). Same person. Same resume. Same qualifications. He was hired on merit, but got the opportunity to interview based on networking.

As you build and maintain relationships, you have an opportunity to provide valuable information for other people, which is key in demonstrating your professional value, increasing your visibility, and enhancing your career. It also reduces the isolation that introverts can tend toward in their pursuit of solitude. In the context of a job search, which can be a roller-coaster ride with deeper and deeper emotional lows, this can be particularly important to counter the depression that can occur.

Completing the Puzzle

Networking occurs whenever people interact with other people. You're already doing it in casual ways, whether you've called it that or not. To apply it more systematically, think about ways that you can increase opportunities to interact with people. These interactions can occur in group contexts or one-on-one. Some of these interactions will have more a defined agenda, but some will simply involve exposure to people in ways that enable you to gain their trust and respect as they get to know you better. You can manage the extent to which you feel in the spotlight simply by redirecting your attention to the needs of those around you. And you can use careful preparation to manage the energy and the stimulation involved in social encounters and to organize your thoughts for smoother conversations. Settings in which networking can occur are listed below, along with some specific techniques for making the most of the opportunities in a way that addresses the needs of those who are introverted or shy.

Where to Network

Group Events

Introverts don't typically enjoy group events, but sometimes they are necessary and unavoidable, both in life generally and in your career specifically. By definition, since you're mingling with people, you will be networking in one form or another because you will be exchanging information. You will also be visible, and your presence will be noted. As Woody Allen said, "Eighty percent of success is showing up." Even events that are not career-related can benefit your career, although you may not always be able to predict or determine precisely how. If you do attend any of these kinds of events, be open to the possibilities. Sometimes simply engaging in an activity with others who share your interest is enough of a connection to begin to build the personal trust that is the foundation of networking. Perhaps you will find it advantageous to deliberately seek out some of these kinds of gatherings or activities either to advance your job search or to further your career.

Specific tips for handling these events will appear in the Strategies section.

Formal networking events

Alumni reunions

Professional association meetings or conferences

Holiday parties, family/neighborhood gatherings

Workshops/seminars

Political, community, or religious activities

Hobbies, sports, clubs, recreational events

Volunteer activities

Individual Communications

The introvert typically prefers one-on-one contacts to large groups, and there are infinite possibilities for these kinds of meetings. They can occur as planned sessions with a specific agenda—such as the information exchange ideas noted in the section above (Wired to Help) or they may be chance encounters and casual conversations. Specific tips for managing energy, self-consciousness, and general awkwardness will appear in the Strategies section.

Social Networking Sites/Internet

To the delight of many who are introverted or shy, there is a growing number of opportunities online to develop relationships that can be beneficial professionally. Social networking sites such as http://linkedin.com, http://facebook.com, and http://twitter.com were mentioned earlier (Chapter 2) as sites that originated to enable people to build and maintain relationships online. Sites such as these can balance the scales for introverts by enabling you to take time to analyze ideas or allow your thoughts to crystallize before sharing them with others. In addition, creating a professional blog or commenting on posts of other bloggers, or even creating a wiki in your area of expertise, provide the same advantage—professional visibility and opportunities to forge connections, with the time to process and reflect before responding. Likewise, you can seek out affinity networks to find other opportunities to form professional connections. As noted before, employers visit these sites to look for promising candidates, so keep your posts appropriate and professional.

Strategies

The strategies presented here are intended to provide new options to try, and to remove some of the discomfort from networking. The purpose is to help you develop the versatility to apply skills that are appropriate to each situation, not to be someone you're not. As you prepare to step outside your comfort zone, remember this quote from Eleanor Roosevelt: "You must do the things you think you cannot do."

Large Gatherings

Before the Event

Prepare—Preparation will make the event flow more easily. Start by preparing a comfortable and brief (say, 30-second) introduction for yourself, since you'll be asked about yourself numerous times. Describe what you do in terms that the listener can relate to—if the other person is from your industry, you can use technical jargon, but if not, tailor your answer to match your audience. You'll want to have a supply of business cards—if you're currently unemployed, you can have business cards created for you with your name, contact information, the job that you're targeting, and perhaps a statement indicating your areas of expertise or personal brand. Next, contact the organizers to find out who else will be there. You can then plan to seek out specific people you would like to meet, enabling you to use your time (and energy) efficiently. You can also do some background research about them beforehand, to make conversation easier. People will be flattered that you know a little about them. Finally, if you need to, prepare general conversation starters, such as those in the chart below. If you dislike superficial chit-chat, remember that these kinds of opening statements or questions get the conversation flowing and can lead to more substantive discussions.

Sample Conversation Starters

You can start a conversation with questions or observations, or a combination of the two. Just taking the initiative is often enough to engage the other person. Here are some topics and sample questions and comments.

The Occasion

- How do you know the host?

- What do you know about tonight's speaker?

- I've never come to this kind of event before. What typically happens?

Location

- This is a beautiful setting. Have you been here before?

- What a view! Those mountains are amazing!

- There was a lot of traffic getting here. Do you know a good way to avoid the highway?

Nametag Information

- That's an interesting name. How do you pronounce it?

- You're from Albuquerque! I've always wanted to go there. How do you like living there?

- [Read company name aloud.] What kind of business is that?

- [Read company name aloud.] How did you come up with that name?

- [Read company name aloud.] How did you get into that line of work?

Visual Cues

- There's quite a good turnout today.

- I love your pin. Is there a story behind it?

- Look at all those tempting desserts.

Topical (but avoid politics)

- I wonder if the weather will discourage people from coming tonight.

- Are you a [sports team] fan? That was a great game last weekend.

Ask Host/Organizer for Help with Introductions—Those who coordinate these events want to be sure they run smoothly, and part of their role is to help connect people. To help get started at a large event, let those in charge know if this is a first-time event for you, or if there's a particular person you would like an introduction to.

Volunteer—Offer to serve on the welcoming committee. Having a role as host redirects your attention to others, which makes you less self-conscious, and it gives others a reason to initiate conversations with you.

Set a Realistic Goal—Determine in advance how many people you think you can reasonably talk with. You aren't obligated to talk with everyone, and you most definitely don't want to attempt to do anything resembling "working the room"—you don't want to be "worked," and neither do the others attending. Decide that you're going to try to talk with, say, three people before the event is over and learn what you can about them. Define success as meeting your goal of three conversations.

Organize Your Day—This one isn't always possible, but if you can schedule your networking activities for the block of time when your energy is highest, the event will be easier. Also, try to plan the rest of your day with lower energy activities so you're not too drained.

Recall Prior Events—Some introverts find it helpful to remember that these events are often not quite as difficult as they fear they will be. Once you're there, it's not so bad. (I sometimes think about networking the way I think about a hot summer's day in New England, wanting to cool off by plunging into the cold Atlantic Ocean, where the water temperature remains quite chilly until well into summer. The initial sensation is unpleasant, but with time, the water feels good.)

During the Event

Arrive Early—When you are one of the first to arrive, people haven't yet begun to form those small groups that can be so hard to break into. Instead, those who are there are likely to glom onto the other early arrivals so that they have someone to talk to.

Take Breaks—If you attend a long or multi-day event, make sure you build in some time for solitude. You may need to pass on some of the group social events, or perhaps skip a workshop or two (if you have the option to do that) so that you can attend the social event. The first few times I attended three-day professional conferences, I thought I needed to get my money's worth and attend every session, but by the end my head was spinning and I could barely absorb what speakers were saying. I learned to be selective in managing time, activities, and energy.

Leave Early—Give yourself permission to leave early if your energy lags. If you combine this strategy with the goal of talking with a select number of people, it is possible to have a successful experience that doesn't leave you depleted.

Bring a Friend—Consider attending with an acquaintance, friend, or colleague. Although you will most likely go separate ways, you'll have the comfort of having a friendly face in the room, a failsafe person to talk with. Variation: Attend with an extraverted friend or colleague, who sometimes can help make introductions.

Look for Other Introverts—Notice others who appear to be on the fringe or who look like they may be stepping back to recharge and engage them in conversation. You may find them similarly receptive to the kind of exchange that you're more interested in. And if they are shy, they will most likely welcome your taking the initiative.

Listen—Use your listening skills to do research about others there—learn about their needs, interests, and challenges (you can jot notes about those on the back of people's business cards, when you exchange cards). This will be useful for the "giving back" part of networking. It's also a handy skill to have when you're with extraverts, because you give them an opportunity to talk—You can make as much of a favorable impression by giving others the spotlight as you can by being a scintillating conversationalist. Finally, you can use your listening skills to connect with other introverts.

After the Event

Follow Up—Send a quick email to each of the people you've spoken with (since you set a reasonable goal in the first place, it can be relatively quick and easy to do this), acknowledging the time they spent with you. If you uncovered any informational needs, send articles or links or names of contacts that address those needs, or offer any further thoughts you may have had on your conversation with them. If you met someone you would like to maintain contact with, you can suggest a more in-depth conversation over coffee or lunch.

One-on-One Contacts

Before You Connect

Keep in Touch—It's helpful, on general principles, to keep in touch with people you know professionally. If you maintain relationships when you don't need anything in particular—just to share information, bounce ideas around, keep up to date on people's career progression and personal lives—it becomes easier to contact people if you do need something. Enjoy the energy flow of one-on-one interactions.

Prepare—Know what your purpose is in contacting people. Most people will want to be helpful, provided you can identify specific ways in which they can help. Develop a clear introduction for yourself so that you can state what you are looking for.

Take the Pressure Off—As with large group events, set goals that are within reach. Perhaps making only two or three phone calls is reasonable for you in one day. Allow yourself recovery time if you need it. Remind yourself that there doesn't have to be a lot riding on the conversation. As one person I spoke with said, "What's the worst that can happen?"

Feel the Fear and Do it Anyway—If you're-anticipating a conversation that makes you uncomfortable, such as contacting someone you don't know, it may help to remember that, in all likelihood, the conversation will be brief, and you can tolerate a brief period of discomfort. The outcome will make the discomfort worth enduring.

Prime the Pump—Several introverts told me that if they had to make difficult phone calls, they found it helpful to make one or two "inconsequential" phone calls beforehand, to sort of warm up and get their thoughts flowing. So they would schedule a hair cut appointment or call a friend, or engage in some kind of simpler conversation before making the important phone call.

Practice—As you repeat some of these activities, even those that seem hard, they become easier.

Bribery—Sometimes you can push yourself to step out of your comfort zone by using good old-fashioned bribery. Set a reasonable goal and reward yourself for achieving it.

Pave the Way—If someone gives you the name of someone to call, ask them to call ahead to make sure their contact is willing to talk with you. It's much easier to contact someone if you know they're willing to receive your call. Or if you know that they prefer to receive an email instead.

While You Connect

Manage the Time—In all of your encounters, keep track of time so that you don't overstay your welcome. Have an agenda, and have a purpose for your conversation.

Shift the Spotlight—If you sincerely focus your attention on what other people need, you'll be less self-conscious about contacting them and during your conversation. If you are calling because of your own need, focus on asking for advice or information. That tends to reduce the fear of rejection, and it reduces the feeling that you're asking for charity. Benjamin Disraeli said, "Talk to people about themselves and they will listen for hours."

Use Email—This doesn't work for everyone, but many introverts expressed a very strong preference for using email rather than the phone, because it allows them time to carefully formulate their thoughts and say exactly what they want to say. Just be sure that your subject line is one that will ensure that the email will be read and not deleted automatically as another piece of junk mail.

After You Connect

Follow Up—Once you've had a conversation with someone, ask if you can touch base with them in a few weeks, or perhaps after you've spoken with someone they've connected you with. Having their permission for another conversation will make it easier for you to follow up with people.

Pay it Forward—One of the aspects of networking that is uncomfortable is that it can feel lopsided when you are the one asking for information or advice and you don't feel you have anything to offer the other person. You may not always be able to give back directly to the person who helped you, but you can carry the spirit of giving forward to help the next person, and do something helpful for someone else who is in need.

Send Thanks—Remember to send a thank you note when people have gone out of their way to provide useful information or contacts. In addition, a sincere thank you following a presentation that you attend is another way to initiate further dialogue and potentially build or expand a relationship.

Quotes

Dan Schawbel, Publisher, Personal Branding Magazine, http://personalbrandingmag.com/staff.htm

"With the rise of web 2.0, the social graph and the growth in participation on the Internet, the introverted can become empowered. Blogs, social networks, virtual worlds and wikis have provided them with shelter for their ideas and relationships. The digital world has become a bootcamp or training ground for introverts."

Lee Ann Lambert, http://blog.hermitshearth.com/2008/03/04/ introvert-job-hunt-revisited.aspx (http://tinyurl.com/5ylfpe)

"Sending an email is a fairly unobtrusive way to get the word out. You need to be certain that your email is very well written and concise, describing what you are looking for… It should highlight your qualifications, but don't overdo it. Just give everyone a good idea of who you are professionally and what you have to offer. I found that upon sending out my email, it was forwarded to others, so that it reached a lot of people.

"Douglas," formerly mechanical engineer, now MBA student/ management consultant

"In b-school, most of the recruiting activities focus around networking events ('meet and greets'). Extraversion abounds! However, if you watch carefully, you can identify the introverts. Was a recruiter talking with several students at once, only to excuse himself/herself to get a drink or snack, and did they then not return to the group? They're probably

'recharging' and you can typically strike up a more private one-on-one conversation with them."

Nancy Loderick, Internet strategist and efficiency expert

"Get involved in activities or organizations that have a meaning for you, whether charity work or, for me, being a mentor. That works. You're doing something you enjoy, people can see you relaxed, doing something that you're really into, and they'll get to know you."

Donna Jean Kaiser, mechanical engineer

"I rely on heavy use of email for networking—it's not in real time, I can check it over, and I don't have to worry about no visual feedback on the phone—I feel more in control."

"For any important phone conversations—I prepare and 'loosen up' my phone comfortableness by calling people for non-important information, setting up appointments, etc. This makes it easier to gain enough momentum where I can call a stranger up to discuss something really important."

Rick Sullivan, director of software engineering, GateRocket, Inc.

"One tactic that seems to work is to engage in a conversation with someone that I know, or that is easy to talk to. This seems to energize the 'conversation center' of my brain (if there's any such thing), and warms me up for a more challenging conversation. Another tactic is to think of all the people that have called me out of the blue as part of a job search. This helps me internalize the fact that it's no big deal, and makes it a little easier."

"Sandy," corporate writing trainer

"I just take a deep breath and force myself to do it and remember that my experience is that once I'm there, it usually works out better than I thought."

"I can go to organizations or meetings or situations with a whole lot of people I don't know, and I know someone who's going—we don't go together or leave together—but I know there's a friendly person in the room, and it helps."

"Marcia," career development facilitator

"Having email makes things so much easier, because you can drop a line to contacts and stay in touch in a very casual, yet straightforward way. I also satisfy my natural curiosity about people and 'what is going on' so I like to keep in touch now."

Claire, social worker

"I had a kind of gut reaction to [networking] which was, I can't imagine calling people up that I didn't know and talking with them. When I reframed what the purposes of the meetings were, then it became kind of interesting. I'm going to learn about a field that maybe I don't know anything much about…I found out that instead of it being intimidating, in fact it was kind of an interesting adventure."

"The other thing that helped was encountering a fair number of people who had themselves done networking and I had people say this to me, which was that when they were doing their own job searches and were networking with people, because they were so appreciative of that, they promised themselves that they would always help other people do that. Kind of like the movie, Pay It Forward. Which actually ended up being how I feel about it at this point. It was interesting how many people articulated that."

"Part of the issue for me was not only how can I ask for people's time, but the other part of the issue was what am I going to ask them. How am I going to meet people that I don't know and keep a conversation going for a half hour. I knew I was going to ask them to get an overview of what they did. I always knew I was going to give them the 60-seconds of my background and ask the question how they would see fitting, in what ways they thought that would prepare me or not for the kind of work that they did… what I would need to do to be a candidate to work in whatever area they were working in. so I sort of had a few things I knew we were going to talk about, and that anchored me."

Jeanne Knight, career and job search coach

"I do tend to be shy, or uncomfortable, in group situations where I don't know people, such as at a cocktail party where everyone is standing around making small talk. What I do in those situations to overcome those feelings of shyness is find someone who is standing all by themselves and go and strike up a conversation with them."

Joshua S. Margolis, CFA, assistant vice president, Martingale Asset Management, L.P.

"Sometimes it took a little mental prep—normally I could prep myself and just go and do it. Take deep breaths, say 'what's the worst that can happen?' Making it feel like a less pressured situation than it was."

5 Promoting Yourself

Interviewing

You've cleared the first hurdle—you've been invited for an interview. This final obstacle stirs up a fair amount of anxiety in most people. You can reassure yourself with a little known fact—a large percentage of the time, interviewers are nervous too! Their managers have placed a lot of expectations on them. They have to make a good selection, stay within budget, and bring someone on board who can fit in and quickly get up to speed. When they hire a stranger, they are taking a risk (which is one of the reasons companies like to hire through referrals)—it costs time and money to hire and train someone—and if they make a bad decision, they may lose out on a good candidate who is hired elsewhere. In addition to this pressure, sometimes interviewers have been given little training on how to interview. As a result, when you come to the interview well prepared, you make their job easier—and that alone can result in their forming a favorable impression of you.

Change the Story

"I'm not good at thinking on my feet."

"I hate the pressure of being judged."

"I worry about having the wrong answer."

"I'm not good at promoting myself."

"I *really* need to get this job!"

The rest of this chapter will discuss reframes of these stories and will present strategies to help you interview effectively.

A Conversation, Not an Interrogation—Bring your curiosity, and think of the interview as a conversation that you're having, not as an interrogation. You're going there to find out as much as you can about the position, the interviewer, the company, your prospective manager, and your coworkers, to assess whether this is a good fit for you. You may really need *a* job, but you may not really need *this* job. Take the pressure off yourself. If you shift the focus of your attention to the employer and what you can learn about it, you will be using your introverted inclination to dig deeper. At the same time, with your focus not on yourself, you will become less nervous and, ultimately, more effective. And if you shift your attention in this way, the emphasis is not on having the right answer or any particular answer at all, but rather on having the right questions.

Level the Playing Field—To extend the above point, the other mental shift you can do is to adopt the view of yourself as consulting with the employer to help him or her determine the best candidate for the position—whether or not that candidate is you.[21] Your goal is to ask questions that clarify for the employer what the key challenges, and—most importantly—what the key outcomes are that are expected of the person hired. By adopting a consulting mindset, you take the performance pressure out of the equation.

"Reporting," not "Bragging"—Just as you're expected to describe your accomplishments on your resume, you are going to need to discuss them in an interview. And just as you used stories to illustrate those accomplishments on the resume, you can tell stories in the interview for the same purpose. You can describe the challenge you were faced with, the steps you took to handle it, and the results you achieved. It's not brag-

---

21. This concept is at the core of the professional speaking model taught by Dean Lincoln Hyers, film director/professional speaker, http://sagepresence.com

ging, just reporting the facts. If you can tap into those stories that you found most satisfying or enjoyable, or those that you're proud of, your natural enthusiasm and excitement will come through. Additionally, if you were raised to believe that it's disrespectful to talk about yourself, consider a different perspective instead, that speaking of your accomplishments is actually an indication that you (1) respect yourself by fully recognizing and appreciating your skills, abilities, and accomplishments, (2) respect your family, by maximizing your ability to provide for them, and (3) respect employers, by providing appropriate information for them to make a good decision.[22]

Chemistry—When you've been called in for an interview, employers have already determined that you have many, if not most, of the essential qualifications. One purpose of the interview is to determine if you will fit in, if the "chemistry" is right (as noted above in "A Conversation, Not an Interrogation," that works both ways, as you seek to determine if the company is a good fit for you). Even if an employer raises some objections or concerns about your background, remember that not everyone gets invited for an interview in the first place—something about your background was of interest. If challenged, you can ask what on your resume attracted them, for example, "I'm wondering what it was on my resume that made you ask me to come in today." Your composure and your ability to develop rapport can offset imperfect answers.

The Grass Isn't Always Greener . . . —If you feel awkward about interviewing and think that extraverts have all the advantages, consider these drawbacks that extraverts as well as hiring managers have shared with me. Because many extraverts tend to formulate their thoughts as they speak, their answers can be rambling and unfocused. And because they converse so easily, they sometimes don't do much preparation and just "wing it," contributing further to answers that are too long-winded. In addition, extraverts sometimes have a tendency to talk before they fully understand the question, or to talk over the interviewer, neither of which scores points, since they can miss the point of the interviewer's question altogether. High-energy extraverts have commented that their exuberance sometimes overpowers or overwhelms people—they come on too strong.

---

22. From the RESPECT™ model for job interviews and performance dialogs, with permission of Murray A. Mann, CCM, CPBS, Principal of Global Diversity Solutions Group, http://GlobalDiversitySolutions.com

Completing the Puzzle

Just as the real estate world emphasizes "location, location, location," interviewing is all about "preparation, preparation, preparation." If you're an introvert, that plays to your strength and gives you an advantage. Being prepared will enable you to manage introversion or shyness and make the interview process easier.

Remember that one of the key goals of the interview is to establish rapport. The stories you tell in the interview will enable you to do that. If you make sure the stories follow the P-A-R format described in Chapter 3, spelling out the problem you faced, the action you took, and the results you achieved, you'll be able to avoid minimalist answers.

As you think about using your introversion to your advantage, think about the many positives that are associated with introversion, and consider ways that you might work those into your conversation. For example, if you're asked to describe your greatest weakness, you can offer a variation on an answer like this: "You'll find at staff meetings that I probably won't be the first one out of the gate to contribute ideas or opinions, but when I do offer my thoughts, they're well thought out and well supported." By referencing your introverted traits in your answers, you're letting the employer know exactly what to expect when you come on board, and you're doing so in a way that puts your introversion in a positive light.

Remember the basics: show up on time, dress professionally, smile and be friendly, have a firm handshake and good eye contact. If at all possible, avoid discussing salary and benefits unless an offer is on the table.

Be prepared for some phone interviews or screenings before an actual in-person interview. These are sometimes scheduled just like a regular face-to-face interview, but many times they're not, and you're caught off guard by a call you weren't expecting. Ask to put the caller on hold for a minute while you take the call in a room where you can talk privately. Even if you're home alone, taking a few minutes to clear your head lets you find your notes about this employer, refresh your memory about the position, and organize your thoughts before actually having to speak. When you pick up the phone again, feel free to ask the caller to repeat whatever information didn't register right away.

Finally, if speaking extemporaneously remains a struggle, consider joining a public speaking group such as Toastmasters or working with a coach on public speaking or interviewing to improve these skills.

Strategies

Before the Interview

Get the Details—When you are invited for an interview, ask about the structure of the interview. How many people will you be meeting with? What are their names and titles? Will you be meeting with them together or in back-to-back meetings? How much time should you schedule for the interview process? Knowing the expected time frame will allow you to manage your energy flow, following the techniques described below. Advance knowledge of the sequence of events will reduce the stress and the energy drain. Also, get directions and parking options and, if you have time, do a trial run to learn the route and check the travel time. These are details that are within your control, and you'll decrease the stress and your overall nervousness on the day of the interview if you get on top of them.

Prepare—Research the Employer and Interviewer—Your introverted preference for in-depth information will serve you really well here, as you gather as much information as you can find about the company, the competition, the industry, and the people you'll be meeting with. Do some research on the company Web site, but also look for information on Google and other sources such as http://zoominfo.com, http://linkedin.com, http://hoovers.com, and business periodicals. Also see what you can find out about the interviewers—search for their names on Google, LinkedIn, and at http://zabasearch.com and http://zoominfo.com. The information you find will be helpful in your conversations. In addition, as an introvert, having time to process that information ahead of the interview will help you prepare answers that match your background with the employer's needs. You will impress the employer with the interest you've taken in doing that background research, since relatively few job seekers take the time to do that.

Prepare—Polish Your Message—In creating your resume, you have identified the most important things you think an employer needs to know about you. Refine that to match specific needs you've uncovered about this particular employer. Review the stories you can tell to support your message. The goal is to develop several brief stories that illustrate the skills and competencies that the employer cares about.

In addition, develop a short statement that summarizes your accomplishments in three to five sentences and describes your value to the employer—this answers the "tell me about yourself" question. Get a list of frequently asked interview questions and prepare answers ahead of time. Anticipate behavioral questions ("tell me about a time . . . ") that examine how you handled problem situations, as well as hypothetical questions ("what would you do if . . . ") that indicate how you think about problems. Consider actually writing out your answers, or rehearsing them out loud with a friend (or a tape recorder), not to memorize the answers, but to engage several of your senses in the process of remembering. Practicing in this manner helps you compensate for word-retrieval issues, helps your confidence, and reduces the likelihood that you'll be caught off guard.

Prepare—Develop Your Questions—Employers expect you to be interested enough to have questions for them. Prepare some questions ahead of time and refer to them at the appropriate time. Not asking questions is interpreted as disinterest. You can ask questions that will reveal whether the general corporate culture is extraverted or introverted. What is a typical day like in your role? Do people eat together or hang out together during or after work? Is most communication in person or by phone, or is it primarily by email? What is your physical environment—in cubes surrounded by others, in a large group environment, in a private office? If offered the job, consider asking to talk with peers or to see where you'll actually be working. Excellent questions to ask are those based on information you learned through your research—let the interviewer know you were interested enough to do some "homework." Other questions you can ask include the following:

"What experience and skills does someone need to be effective in this job?"

"What's the first problem you need the person you hire to tackle?"

"At the end of six months, what needs to be accomplished?"

"How will that be measured? How will you know whether it's been accomplished?"

Also, be sure to ask about the next steps in the process at the conclusion of the interview.

During the Interview

Allow Yourself Time to Think—If you're asked a question that you don't have an immediate answer for, it's acceptable to say, "That's a good question. Let me think about that for a minute." Then sit silently for a moment and organize your thoughts. By announcing that you need a minute to think, you've given a response right away, even though you haven't yet given your answer. Essentially, you've bought yourself some time and slowed down the process.

Use a "Cheat Sheet"—If you're concerned that you'll forget the examples you came up with during your advance preparation, bring a leather-bound notepad with you, and use the paper both to take notes and to prepare ahead of time a couple of words or phrases as cues to your stories. (These cues need to be very brief, or else you'll have trouble finding the information on the page.) Then, during your momentary pause to organize your thoughts, you can glance down at your notepad and find the prompts you've written for yourself. This strategy can help you think on your feet.

Sometimes Your Work *Can* Speak For Itself—Bring a portfolio with you that displays samples of your work, certifications, honors and awards, testimonials, and so on. You can redirect the interviewer's attention onto the portfolio and show what you can produce.

Let Others Speak for You—If you've made a positive impression on others, whether clients, managers, coworkers, or others who know your professional work, you can reference what they said about your work. When a question comes along that invites a strong statement on your behalf and you worry about sounding boastful, you can say, "My clients consistently commented that . . . " or "In my performance evaluation, my manager wrote . . . "

Shift the Spotlight—You can refocus the spotlight and take the pressure off yourself by concentrating on learning as much as you can about the company and the interviewer(s). Being curious about the organization and people you're meeting with will divert your attention from yourself, reducing self-consciousness and enhancing your effectiveness.

Reframe Your Introverted Information Processing Style as a Strength—Because we live in a society that values extraverted behaviors, you may have come to regard your slower thought processing as a flaw. On the contrary, your careful deliberation and analysis means your answers will be well thought out—introverts don't "shoot from the hip." If you're called upon to describe a strength, consider identifying this quality and presenting it as the strength that it is. This has the added benefit of alerting the interviewer to your introverted style, to provide a context for your more methodical manner.

Manage Your Energy—If you have a marathon interview that involves multiple interviewers and many hours, you may begin to feel depleted. Ask for a bathroom break, just to give yourself a moment alone and a chance to regroup. If need be, have an energy bar. You can also use this opportunity to glance again at any notes you've brought with you.

Show Enthusiasm—If the job interests you, say so. Employers want to hire people who are genuinely enthusiastic about the job. One Human Resources manager told me that he almost didn't hire someone because she showed so little excitement about the position. He hired her only because she came with a strong referral—without that, he would never have offered her the position. A good place to express your interest is at the conclusion of the interview; along with thanking the interviewer, state your continued interest in the position and reiterate in a sentence or two the match between your background and the requirements.

Redefine Success—You're not in control of the outcome of an interview; you're only in control of your ability to deliver a clear message about who you are and what you have to offer. Find an opportunity to convey your message. You almost always can do it at the beginning of the interview, in response to the "tell me about yourself" question, which usually occurs in the first few minutes. You can do it if you're asked a question such as "Why should we hire you?" And you can do it as part of your wrap-up at the end of the interview as you thank the interviewer and repeat the reasons you believe you qualify for the position. If you've delivered your message at any (or all) of these points in the interview, consider yourself successful, whether or not you are offered the job.

After the Interview

Send a Thank You Letter—Always send an individual letter of thanks to each person you speak with. In addition to demonstrating common courtesy, you have an opportunity to reinforce a point you thought was well received or to restate your message. Or, in the event you seriously stumble over an answer, you have an opportunity to recover by noting that, on further reflection about a particular question, you have additional thoughts, and then briefly state them.

Create a Hypothetical Action Plan—You can apply your introverted and analytical skills by proposing a hypothetical action plan that outlines steps you would take if you were hired—and send that along with your thanks. Not only does this strategy "go the extra mile," it enables the employer to visualize you in the role that you're applying for.

Quotes

Meghan Wier, business writer/author: Confessions of an Introvert, The Shy Girl's Guide to Career, Networking and Getting the Most Out of Life

"As an introvert, the interview itself is not as much of a problem/challenge as the time before and after. I always have to take quiet time before and after to calm myself."

Barbie Dallman, certified Professional Life Coach, http://CoachBarbie.com

"The best skill I developed was going to Toastmasters and participating in Table Topics—extemporaneous talking—The skill was how to think and talk simultaneously."

"Often I will ask a question back. Let them talk a little while. Or ask them to explain, 'What do you mean by . . . ?' Or talk about the question: 'That's a really good question; that's something I've thought about for a while.'"

"I think it is really important to move from that place where I want everybody to like me and accept me to a place where I want to show up being the me that's going to show up at the job. So it's a good match. Because every job I apply for isn't going to be a good match."

"The interview is a two-way street. You have to find out if you want to work there. Come with curiosity."

Dean Lincoln Hyers, film director / professional speaker, http://sagepresence.com

"I used to be stopped dead in my tracks—just being asked. I drew a complete blank. I've gotten extremely good under pressure, in the hot seat. Practice was part of it . . . I think practice, being in the hot seat, is a lot of it. Public speaking is a lot of it—forces me to get in the hot seat, deal with questions, be prepared."

"When performance pressure leads you to pay attention to you, performance diminishes. The practice that gets you out of that is appreciating something outside of you."

Dianne, dental assistant, medical researcher

"In job search—I dislike talking about myself, promoting myself; I'd rather let my actions or deeds speak for themselves. I really dislike promoting myself and telling people why I'm so great. I would use examples of what I had done in the past and then I would create imaginary situations and explain how I might handle them if it came up. I also tended to take the offense instead of the defense; it wouldn't just be asking me questions, but I would be digging from them as well. It wouldn't be a one-way street; it would be a two-way street, and hopefully from what I would delve into, they would garner some information about me. So it became more of a discourse than just an interrogation."

Donna Jean Kaiser, mechanical engineer

"I enjoyed interviews—always something interesting going on to learn. Listen to the other person and ask questions—easy because so many things are interesting."

Dr. Terrie Wurzbacher, author of *Your Doctor Said What?*

"A big part of the fear . . . if you don't think you're very worthy . . . part of the fear of calling or going on an interview—they're going to see right through me. But once I'm in the job, I can show you through my performance."

Jeanne Knight, career and job search coach

"When it comes to interviewing, what I've done is force myself to be outside of my comfort zone . . . almost like I've put on an 'act' for the duration of the interview. I become outwardly enthusiastic and upbeat, talkative and inquisitive. I find that the less I actually think about the interview, the easier it is for me to go out of my comfort zone like that."

Joshua S. Margolis, CFA, assistant vice president, Martingale Asset Management, L.P.

"I tried to go in with the attitude that it wasn't the end of the world if I didn't get the job, that there would be other things coming along."

"Thank you notes were a big thing, being aggressive with follow-up calls, not being afraid to call and show your interest."

Murray A. Mann, CCM, CPBS, Principal of Global Diversity Solutions Group, LLC, http://GlobalDiversitySolutions.com

"My nature and upbringing was to be respectful and not talk about myself. Turn that on it's head and say it's disrespectful not to. Go to your immediate family or important people in your life and ask, 'What are you proud of me for?' Embrace their acknowledgment of your accomplishments as permission to talk about them with employers. Continuing to expand your comfort zone by asking the same question to your friends, coworkers, teachers, mentors, supervisors and others, will improve your confidence."

Wayne Purnell, organizational consulting

"I try not to take things personally. It's not helpful to think of it as rejection—that can become a self-fulfilling prophecy and can sabotage the next interview."

"In an interview, I'm perceived as laid back, not high energy, so in preparing for interviews, I'll sort of get myself up and say my normal style is not going to be real helpful. I'm going to be prepared to go in with a somewhat higher energy. Get myself up and appear more animated."

"For somebody who is more introverted, because they tend to clarify by thinking about things, they could be perceived as non-responsive or non-interactive, and what I would do is say, 'I'm going to think about that for a minute.' Say that I'm going to be more reflective, I'm going to be thoughtful, rather than leave them to wonder about why I'm being quiet."

Kathy Scarpone, administrative specialist

"I find that taking notes during an interview is crucial for me. Many times my questions are based on the notes I've taken. But I always do my home-work up front (checking the company website, etc.) so I'm prepared with written questions."

"Use your introversion to be prepared. Take great notes. Document your job search. Be organized and methodical about what your skills are."

Rick Sullivan, director of software engineering, GateRocket, Inc.

"Introversion may enhance my enthusiasm for reading and researching possible job opportunities. I enjoy researching companies that interest me, and can usually generate quite a bit of enthusiasm—which is a huge help in the interview process."

"The best advice I have for a job interview is to come well armed with knowledge of the company, and to demonstrate interest and enthusiasm. . . . Preparation helps—reading about the company, talking to others who work there, etc. etc."

6 After You Land— Transitioning to Success

As you prepare to start a new job, you have the opportunity to think about what you can do to make the transition easier. Not only will you be learning a new job in a new organization, but you'll be learning how to fit into the culture and build professional relationships in the new organization.

First Impressions

Acclimating to a new job is exciting but also stressful. The edge you have as an introvert is your ability to listen and learn the ropes. Use the "honeymoon" period to get to know your coworkers: their roles, their history with the company, their perceptions of office politics (be careful to keep your own objectivity and just mentally record their observations without taking them to heart), and so on. Your genuine interest in others will go a long way toward making a good first impression and building solid professional relationships. As with the job search process, focusing your attention on others will relieve any early jitters you may feel.

Adjust to the Environment

If you're an introvert in an extraverted environment, you can adopt a number of different strategies to accommodate your need for concentration, solitude, and the like. Perhaps you can substitute email for phone conversations for some of your communications. You may want to consider developing a signal or a sign to alert others when you prefer not to be interrupted—but make sure you come up for air and socialize some of the time. Take breaks when you can. Go for walks, go to the restroom, go to your car. Find the solitude you need to recharge. If others in the company typically eat together, you can excuse yourself and explain that you need to recharge, or you can join the group and recharge later. One introvert told me she joins the group but deliberately chooses only to listen. If you're shy, challenge yourself to approach at least one new person each day (or some similar goal)—as you practice your social skills, you will get more comfortable with them.

Meetings and other large gatherings can create challenges for introverts. Ask for the meeting agenda ahead of time so you can review the issues and prepare your thoughts. If you make the time to do so, you'll be able to contribute to the discussion more easily. Several introverts shared with me the frustrating experience of not offering an idea because it wasn't fully formed or because they weren't sure whether it was really a good idea or not, only to have someone else present the same idea and receive lots of praise and recognition for it. Alternatively (or additionally), ask for the option to offer input after you've had time to process the information. Follow-up with an email that summarizes your reactions after you've had time to reflect.

Conscious Communication

Because introverts can so easily withdraw into their work, it's a good idea to pay attention to deliberately communicating with others. It may help to share your style with others so they don't make negative assumptions about your personality or motives. When you get caught up in your thoughts, you can lose sight of the fact that others don't know what you're thinking unless you share those thoughts. (I learned that painful lesson in graduate school when the seven members of a seminar were asked what grades we would give ourselves; I was unpleasantly surprised that the professor didn't agree that I deserved an A—his comment to me was that I may have gotten a lot out of the class, but that wasn't apparent in terms of my contributions to the discussion.) If you concentrate heavily on just the tasks of the job and don't socialize at all, your behavior appears secretive and suspicious to those who prefer high levels of interaction. Pay attention to whether you have a tendency to get so caught up in your thoughts that others don't know what you're thinking.

Just as you need to take breaks from extraverted activities, you'd be wise to take breaks from the intense introverted activities you'll be drawn into. Seek out others to socialize with. This can be superficial conversation about last night's sports event, if that fits the culture of the organization, or it can be more substantive and work-related. Share what you've been working on and get input or advice from others. Most organizations want to know that you can function as part of a team and interact well with others, whatever your individual contribution may be.

Self-Promotion/Visibility

Effective self-promotion helped you to get the job in the first place, and it will help you to advance in your career. A tool that can make this process considerably simpler is an accomplishment journal or log. On a regular basis, record your accomplishments as they occur. While they're fresh in your mind, you can capture all the P-A-R information (described in Chapter 3) that will be valuable if you request promotions, bonuses, or special assignments. A Human Resources manager told me about an engineer, raised in another country, who became discouraged watching others less qualified and less talented receive all the perks—and the primary reason was that he was reluctant to promote himself. Introverts often think their work will speak for itself—but much of the time you have to direct people's attention to the work before they can "hear" what the work has to say. And that's where the accomplishment log can be useful. In addition, when the time comes to update your resume, you'll simplify that process by having all the information you need at hand.

Keep copies of work samples, if appropriate, along with testimonials and performance appraisals, as well, to give additional evidence and support for your future discussions.

Discuss with your manager what arrangement will be mutually comfortable so that you and your work remain visible and the communication channels remain open. Consider partnering with an extravert, someone who will enjoy presenting the ideas but may not relish the in-depth analysis. Extraverts can become powerful allies.

Partner with Others

Sometimes collaborating with others, particularly others who are more extraverted, can pay off as well. You may find that there are people around with skills that complement yours. Look for opportunities to team up and support each other's efforts.

Quotes

Susan Whitcomb, author and career coach

"Try to buy some prep time when thinking about important things...e.g., Ask people to provide you with an agenda of an upcoming important meeting so you've got time to think through what you might want to say. Or, when someone asks, 'What are your thoughts on that?' don't be afraid to say, 'You know, I have some initial thoughts on that and they are [fill in the blank].' And, to be honest, as an introvert, I usually come up with my best ideas about 8 hours later, so I'll be sure and include those thoughts in an email if you'd like!"

"Douglas," formerly mechanical engineer, now MBA student/ management consultant

"I make a conscious effort to be more visible, stopping by the offices of coworkers (even when I don't want to), and learning about their personal lives. I also routinely schedule meetings—hard to believe for an introvert! You have to make a conscious effort to engage people and raise your visibility."

"Another good tactic is to find a salesperson! I try to build a close friend with an extravert who can take of tasks that require, well, more extraversion. I'm not comfortable being visible or 'in the limelight.' Therefore, I typically team with a leader who will deliver my messages in more appropriate ways."

Nancy Loderick, Internet strategist and efficiency expert

"In B-school, I remember thinking I'm not going to say something, it sounds stupid, but then the man next to me says it, and it's a wonderful idea. I

could have said that! It's the same thing in a meeting. I used to think if you keep your head down and do a good job, you'll get recognized. It doesn't work that way."

Jay, college professor

"One thing I tell my class is that introverts are likely to come back with more information—don't think they weren't paying attention. I tell those who aren't introverts to understand that, and those that are that it doesn't hurt to make that explicit, alert your work group that (a) you're unlikely to, won't be the highest participator in terms of words spoken per person and (b) you often need time to go off and think about it and come back. You might set a norm that we don't make decisions until the second meeting and have patience for people."

"Find someone who's an extravert who can lead the way for you."

"Sandy," corporate writing trainer

"After I teach, after any meeting, I come home and I quietly write my notes up. I do that all the time, I write down what happened, what I thought, and what my follow-up is."

Deb Dib, CEO career strategist, http://ExecutivePowerBrand.com

" . . . having a place where you can recharge—even if you have to go to the ladies room and sit there for 10 minutes."

"Marcia," career development facilitator

"Some mornings can be jarring, as I enter the office, maybe with bright fluorescent lights, noise, and cheerful or talkative people, ready to chat. Sometimes I feel almost a physical need to be alone and have more privacy. This is when work seems less about the work one actually performs, and more about how one fits in socially. I can make it clear to others that I am busy by concentrating on the computer, typing, or making some calls I need to make."

"Accept and acknowledge that…you will need to make accommodations for yourself and for others. If someone is noisy or chatty with or around me, I can be or look very busy. Or, I can say, 'I want to talk more about his later, I need to catch up on some work today.'"

"Also, I need to remember that I too like to talk, socialize, and convey my thoughts and feelings; sometimes just less so than some others. Therefore, I need to get out of the comfort zone of thinking that I am being put upon."

Murray A. Mann, CCM, CPBS, Principal of Global Diversity Solutions Group, LLC, http://GlobalDiversitySolutions.com

"I've developed the habit, if I don't want to go [to a networking function], I tell myself that this is what business is all about. Just doing it and not being visible, establishing the credibility—the presence was important. I could be credible in my research but I couldn't be successful without creating the visibility. So I just had to do it."

"I think about: What do I need to accomplish for the project that I'm working on or for the issue I'm passionate about. It's never about me. And that's what made it palatable."

Kathy Scarpone, administrative specialist

"I have lost a few promotions because of my inability to speak up in a meeting and promote my ideas. Many times the extravert will bring up ideas and get credit for those ideas (those same ideas I had for weeks but my introversion held me back—didn't want to sound stupid or have an idea that didn't have merit)."

"I often document my ideas and send emails to my boss or I'll check with a friend to see if my idea sounds good."

Rick Sullivan, director of software engineering, GateRocket, Inc.

"I have a few strategies for forcing interactions with people at work. When I've had management jobs, I've required weekly or bi-weekly one on one meetings with my direct reports...I frequently think of questions to ask co-workers, or small favors to ask them, just to keep the communication flowing. I'll often ask my boss for advice...Besides encouraging communication, this sends the strong message that I value his (or her) opinion."

Section III
Final Thoughts

Chapter

7 | Embrace Your Introversion

It can be challenging to be an introvert in an extra-verted culture, but there are benefits, as well. The more we can appreciate our own introversion, the more others will value it as well. This last chapter will summarize some of the advantages that other intro-verts have described, in the hope that you will recog-nize the many strengths that you bring with you.

I expect that you will find that many of these advan-tages apply to you, but some may not. We are indi-viduals, not a uniform and consistent group. By the same token, some of these advantages will apply to extraverts, who also do not comprise a homoge-neous group. My purpose in presenting these final thoughts is once again to provide some reframes. If you've been "beating yourself up" or "feeling guilty" (in the words of two of the people I interviewed) because of who you are or how you are, there is another way to look at the picture.

Some of the adjectives that frequently come up in describing introverts are quiet, serious, calm, reserved, detached, restrained, and private.[23] All of these speak to our inner focus, and they can

23. There's an excellent discussion of introverted lead-ership traits in Shoya Zichy, *Women and the Leadership Q*, McGraw-Hill, NY, 2001.

contribute to success when used appropriately. In fact, our contemplative nature enables us to very easily practice "Habit 5" of Stephen R. Covey's *The Seven Habits of Highly Effective People: "Seek First to Understand, Then to Be Understood."*[24] We listen well, don't dominate the conversation, and as a result, we give extraverts the space to talk. In addition, we typically get to the point and are less likely to waste time with extraneous conversation, with the dual benefit of being respectful of others' time constraints and being highly productive. Our ideas are well thought out and usually worth listening to when we do share them—we offer quality vs. quantity. We can use our keen listening skills to build deep relationships, which is an essential element in professional endeavors. Others may perceive us as fair, thoughtful, intelligent, competent, diligent, and trustworthy. Our need to process information before speaking means we are less likely than extraverts to say something we will regret, which can be beneficial for those in a high visibility role. Similarly, we are likely not to act too hastily because of the wish to reflect first. The careful preparation that we do not only enables us to function at our optimum, it also inspires confidence on the part of others in the quality of what we do.

It's not always apparent to the outside observer whether you are introverted or extraverted—after all, to be overly simplistic, extraverts think, and introverts talk. Just as with right- or left-handedness, we all have some degree of skill on our non-dominant side. The distinction stems primarily from the energy source. Introverts are energetic when they're involved with the ideas that excite them. They are outgoing when they're connecting with people they care about, especially in one-on-one situations.

The highly social nature of the job search process and the world of work can be over-stimulating to us if we're introverts and taxing to us if we're shy or reserved in nature or if we've been taught that talking about our accomplishments is wrong. And yet there are countless people, some famous and some not, who are successful despite, and sometimes because of, their introverted and more modest traits. The key is to develop the versatility to apply whichever skills are appropriate to achieve your goals—and to make choices that value, appreciate, and, most importantly, celebrate the unique combination of qualities that make you who you are.

I wish you great success in your endeavors.

---

24. Stephen R. Covey, *The Seven Habits of Highly Effective People*, Free Press, NY, 2004, p. 235.

Quotes

Paul Viau, business development manager for technology company

"When I first got into sales and marketing, [introversion] brought forth my technical knowledge and my ability to talk to people and be credible. Being a good listener made me a good sales person. I'm viewed as a thoughtful, intelligent person, someone who's fair-minded."

Susan Whitcomb, author and career coach

"[Introversion] helps me to create the models, ideas, acronyms, insights that I'm known for. It also helps my relationships and ability to connect with others—when I'm talking to someone, I can concentrate on the person fully and not get distracted by other people or activity in the room."

Meghan Wier, business writer/author: *Confessions of an Introvert, The Shy Girl's Guide to Career, Networking and Getting the Most Out of Life*

"I think that as an introvert I know to take time for myself, to be thoughtful and direct. I think before I speak or do (at least I try to!)."

Ann Lawthers, senior director, evaluation and measurement

"I seem to have the gift for listening to complex and winding conversations and reducing them down to their essence. I am also very good at listening to staff and honing in on what their issue or problem is."

"Douglas," formerly mechanical engineer, now MBA student/ management consultant

"'Silent waters run deep.' 'The strong, silent type.' These can be advantageous and project an image of seriousness, diligence, and competence. Also, even though it may seem obvious, if you're not out socializing the whole time you're at work, you can get a lot more done!"

Barbie Dallman, certified Professional Life Coach, http://CoachBarbie.com

"The analytical, deep thinking part is very helpful. Attention to detail, problem solving, brainstorming."

Dianne, dental assistant, medical researcher

"I'm so comfortable being this way. I think it's kept me out of office politics to a great extent. A lot of people would consider me a go-to person because they knew I wasn't going to be talking freely. I think typically being an introvert in the office, I think I'm a lot more observant, a little keener observer of people's personalities."

Jay, college professor

"People experience me as straightforward and not exaggerated...People can appreciate that you're not hogging all the air time. Generally what you say is because it's been thought through a little more; there's a higher ratio of signal to noise. It's more likely to be worth listening to."

"Sandy," corporate writing trainer

"Over time I developed a reputation for careful thinking and planning and fairness and trustworthiness."

Deb Dib, CEO career strategist, http://ExecutivePowerBrand.com

"I think I have an ability to focus more intently on things, to see deeper. You get to see sides of people, take the time and have the desire to see sides of people that for other people might slide by."

Murray A. Mann, CCM, CPBS, Principal of Global Diversity Solutions Group, LLC, http://GlobalDiversitySolutions.com

"I think my introversion allows me to stay focused to do the research and the writing of the work and then to start talking about it."

Rick Sullivan, director of software engineering, GateRocket, Inc.

"My job has a heavy emphasis on analysis and design. I have to spend a lot of time investigating various approaches for solving specific problems...I love this kind of work, and I feel that my introspective nature is a huge advantage. Because of my quiet, introspective nature, I've been perceived as a 'deep thinker.' Whether true or not, this perception has often worked in my favor."

Kathy Scarpone, administrative specialist

"My father always told me that we are born with 2 ears and 1 mouth. It is more important to listen than to talk. We always learn more by listening."

About the Author

Wendy Gelberg is the owner of Gentle Job Search/ Advantage Resumes. She is a certified career coach and resume writer whose expertise is in helping people who are uncomfortable "tooting their own horn." Designated the "Job-Hunt Pro for Introverts" for http://job-hunt.org, Wendy coaches individuals, gives workshops and writes articles and blogs on all aspects of the job search process. Samples of her resumes and career advice appear in over 20 books. Wendy has owned her business for over 10 years. She has been an introvert all her life. Contact Wendy at wendy@gentlejobsearch.com.

About the Author

Recommended Happy About® Books

Purchase these books at Happy About
http://happyabout.info
or at other online and physical bookstores.

Blitz the Ladder

Unique approach to improve
your career
'Blitz the Ladder' will provide you
an in-depth view at a unique
approach to improving
your career.

Paperback: $19.95
(with 15% discount only $16.96)
eBook: $11.95

Internet Your Way to a New Job

From selecting the most effective
tools, to proven methodologies
and expert perspectives, this
book will prepare you to
enter a competitive
job market with confidence.

Paperback: $19.95
(with 15% discount only $16.96)
eBook: $11.95

Happy About My Resume

This book is for anyone who wants to proactively manage their career and improve the quality of their current resume or create a resume from scratch."

Paperback: $19.95
eBook: $11.95

They Made It!

How Chinese, French, German, Indian, Israeli and other foreign born entrepreneurs contributed to high tech innovation in the Silicon Valley, the US and Overseas.

Paperback: $24.95
(with 10% discount only $22.45)
eBook: $11.95

Additional Endorsements

"This is one of the most inspiring books I've read in a long time. The techniques, tactics and stories make this a rich, must-read for anyone who feels like they should be more outgoing, but isn't quite sure how to do it, or if they are being dishonest with themselves."
Jason Alba, CEO, http://JibberJobber.com

"If you cringe at the thought of networking and 'selling yourself,' there is no better guide for your job search than Wendy Gelberg. Wendy provides empathetic advice and practical strategies that will help any introverted or shy person not only be more successful, but feel more confident, assured, and 'normal.' 'The Successful Introvert' is an invaluable guide that is long overdue."
Louise Kursmark, Author, "30-Minute Resume Makeover" and 20 other career books; President, Best Impression Career Services, Inc.

"If you're an introvert, you need this book! Because Gelberg truly understands the introverted personality, you will find great relief and sage advice for managing a job search in this seemingly extroverted world we live (and compete) in."
Susan Ireland (http://susanireland.com), Author, 'The Complete Idiot's Guide to the Perfect Resume'

Printed in the United States
218490BV00005B/27/P

9 781600 051074